Greater Yell

The National Park and Ad

NUMBER SIX

BY RICK REESE

PUBLISHED BY

Montana Magazine, Inc.

HELENA, MONTANA 59604

RICK GRAETZ, PUBLISHER
MARK THOMPSON, PUBLICATIONS DIRECTOR
CAROLYN CUNNINGHAM, EDITOR

This series intends to fill the need for in-depth information about Montana subjects. The geographic concept explores the historical color, the huge landscape and the resilient people of a single Montana subject area. Design by Len Visual Design, Helena, Montana. All camera prep work and layout production completed in Helena, Montana. Typesetting by Thurber Printing, Helena, Montana. Color Lithography — Dai Nippon, San Francisco. Printed in Japan.

The swift metamorphosis and the onward march of civilization, sweeping ever westward, and transforming and taming our wilderness, fills us with a strange regret, and we rejoice that parts of that wilderness will yet remain to us unchanged. Amid our glorious mountains, snowcrowned and towering to the clouds, sheltering in their rocky embrace so many beautiful parks, broad basins and rich valleys, we can yet recall the charm of the old wilderness we once knew.

WILLIAM S. BRACKETT
PARK COUNTY, MT. 1900

Preface

In the pages that follow I have attempted to develop five themes: (1) Yellowstone National Park is a very special, and in some respects, a unique place; (2) the park is not an island, but rather exists in an ecological context that we call the Greater Yellowstone area; (3) the entire Greater Yellowstone Ecosystem is an extraordinary national treasure existing as the largest, essentially-intact ecosystem remaining in the temperate zones of the earth; (4) most resource management decisions in the Greater Yellowstone Ecosystem are made in a fragmented manner, which does not recognize the area as a single ecological unit, but rather views it as more than two dozen separate political and administrative entities; (5) and that the Greater Yellowstone Ecosystem is imperiled by activities and developments that pose imminent threats to its environmental integrity.

I have not directly approached the question of how much development is desirable on the lands of Greater Yellowstone, but my personal bias clearly favors maintaining in a natural condition as much of the entire ecosystem as we possibly can. But no matter how we as individuals or as a nation answer the question of what is an acceptable degree of development for Greater Yellowstone, we must recognize that there will be trade-offs. If we opt to give up more of our wild lands in Greater Yellowstone, we should do it with the full recognition of what will be gained and what will be lost. We should acknowledge that the impacts at one point in the ecosystem also will be felt elsewhere in the area and in ways we can't always predict. We must also proceed in a manner that allows us to openly assess the

A lone bison suns himself in Yellowstone's Hayden Valley. (Tom Dietrich)

trade-offs, on a local as well as on an ecosystem-wide scale.

For most of the three centuries that we have occupied North America, we have operated on the assumption that the earth has been endowed with natural resources to serve only man, who consumes without regard for other living creatures or even for the people of future generations. That attitude often has led us to focus only on the gains to be realized from natural resource exploitation with no real understanding of the corresponding losses. Frequently, costs in the form of degraded land became apparent only after it was too late.

Today in the face of the stark reality that we are finally down to the very last remnants of wild land in our country, a new attitude is more appropriate; an attitude that recognizes that our Creator, in providing us the earth, gave to man a unique gift, an island of habitability in a universe of hostile space, a planet so delicate, so irreplaceable and so fundamental to the survival of the only life we know, that it merits our stringent stewardship and nurturing. In this view conservation, not consumption, should be the driving force of society, maintaining to the highest possible degree the natural face of our fragile planet. By this reckoning, drilling and mining the wilderness, logging the shrinking habitat of threatened species, poisoning our waterways, destroying the great bear and diminishing our park lands have no place. We are not yet that poor as a nation.

Rick Reese

Greater Yellowstone

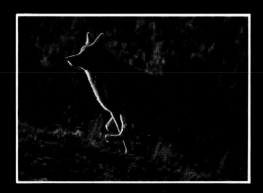

Acknowledgment

The scientific concept of the Greater Yellowstone Ecosystem first came to my attention through a series of evening conversations in 1981 with the late John Townsley, Superintendent of Yellowstone National Park from 1975 to 1982. I gratefully acknowledge the influence which this man's keen intellect and deep dedication to the principles of conservation have had on me during the writing of this book.

Rick Reese

Montana Magazine, Inc.
Box 5630, Helena, MT 59604
ISBN 0-938314-08-4

THE NATIONAL PARK AND ADJACENT WILDLANDS

Contents

Opposite Page: Coyote. (Ron Shade)
Left: Sunrise over Slough Creek. (Tom Murphy)

About the Author:

Rick Reese has served as director of the Yellowstone Institute for the past four years. He was a principal founder of the Greater Yellowstone Coalition and currently serves on the board of that organization. He worked for the National Park Service as a climbing ranger in Grand Teton National Park for a number of years. Reese is the author of the first volume in the Montana Geographic Series, Montana Mountain Ranges.

Introduction

There is a place high astride the Continental Divide in the northern Rocky Mountains of western America where within a few miles of one another the first trickles of the Snake, the Yellowstone and the Green rivers are born. From here everything goes down: to the Columbia, to the Missouri, to the Colorado and on to the sea. During the exploration of the west, this place, where present-day Montana, Idaho and Wyoming converge, was the last major piece to be fitted into the giant puzzle of American geography.

By the time a definitive exploration of the Yellowstone region finally was accomplished in 1871, the remainder of the west was largely settled: the Mormons had been in Utah for more than 20 years, the valleys of the west were being farmed and ranched, John Wesley Powell had explored and mapped the Grand Canyon and the Colorado River, the California gold rush had come and gone, and the fires of the Civil War had been cold for half a decade. A few white men had penetrated the region; one, John Colter of the Lewis and Clark expedition, had walked alone through here in search of furs as early as 1807. Intermittently for the next 60 years an occasional trapper, prospector or explorer would make his way into what mountain men and explorers loosely called The Yellowstone, and a few would even chronicle it as did Osborne Russell, who wrote so eloquently of the area in the 1830s. However, by the latter third of the 19th century, the region of the upper Yellowstone was still essentially terra incognita.

In 1860 an able expedition of the Corps of Topographic Engineers under the leadership of Captain William F. Raynolds made an attempt at an organized exploration of the Yellowstone region, but the expedition failed to penetrate even the outer reaches of the area that today comprises Yellowstone National Park. It was another nine years before three

Hayden expedition campsite on the shore of Yellowstone Lake, 1871. (Wm. H. Jackson, courtesy of the National Park Service)

curious adventurers, David E. Folsom, Charles W. Cook and William Peterson, set out in the fall of 1869 from near Helena in Montana Territory to conduct their own exploration. It was only upon the return of these three to civilization after nearly a month of plying Yellowstone's inner recesses that a comprehensive understanding of the area began to emerge.

Armed with the invaluable information of the Cook-Folsom-Peterson expedition and encouraged by their findings and success, another expedition to Yellowstone under the leadership of Henry D. Washburn, Surveyor General of Montana Territory, was launched from Helena in 1870. This group, consisting of a military escort and 19 persons including several of considerable wealth and political influence, covered much of the ground that Cook, Folsom and Peterson had seen the year before. In addition, Washburn and his party traveled deep into the southeast portion of Yellowstone nearly circumscribing Yellowstone Lake. Upon their return, various members of the expedition wrote articles about the upper Yellowstone and attracted considerable national attention to the wonders they had seen. One of their number, Nathaniel P. Langford, went forth to deliver a series of lectures including one in January 1871 in Washington D.C. Dr. Ferdinand D. Hayden, head of the U.S. Geological Survey of the Territories, was in the audience. Out of this contact between Langford and Hayden were sown the seeds of the famous Hayden Survey of Yellowstone in 1871, the most productive, definitive and elaborate of all the Yellowstone expeditions.

Hayden assembled a large and talented scientific party of geologists, zoologists, botanists and a variety of others including photographer William H. Jackson and artist Thomas Moran. His highly successful expedition

Jupiter Terrace, Mammoth Hot Springs. (Charles Kay)

gathered hundreds of specimens in addition to producing a wealth of notes, photographs and artistic sketches and confirmed the wonders of Yellowstone, which up to that time were largely unverified.

In Washington, Hayden set about compiling his findings in an official report that joined others in urging Congress to set aside the Yellowstone region as America's first national park. That was accomplished just a few short months later when in March 1872, President Grant signed into law an act creating Yellowstone National Park.

In 1872 the vast wilderness of the west was viewed by most Americans as something to be tamed, to be explored, settled, mined, logged, ranched and farmed. For most at that time the west was not valued for its wilderness, but rather for the material treasures that it could.yield. It is remarkable that during such an age Yellowstone was set aside as the world's first national park. That such a park could have been created more than a century ago is perhaps the most illustrative indicator of how unique and magnificent the Yellowstone country was perceived to be, even then.

Of the undisturbed, ecologically cohesive areas that were so common in western America in 1872, few remain. Now, at a time when the face of the earth has become so ravaged

that few truly natural areas remain, the Yellowstone country assumes a value far greater than the original proponents of the national park ever could have anticipated. Here we find the largest essentially intact ecosystem remaining in the lower 48 states—millions of acres of diverse mountain wilderness relatively untouched by the imprint of man, much the same as it was hundreds, or even thousands of years ago. Here in Yellowstone National Park and in the surrounding millions of acres of national forest nearly every species of plant and animal life that John Colter could have seen when he ventured into the area almost 200 years ago continue to flourish.

But Yellowstone National Park is not an island. Geographically, biologically and ecologically it is part of and highly dependent upon millions of acres of adjacent lands, which together with the park itself comprise the "Greater Yellowstone" area. The environmental integrity of Yellowstone Park is dependent upon the careful management of these lands. In most instances the lands around Yellowstone must remain in a relatively natural condition for the biological community of Yellowstone itself to remain viable. Plants and animals do not recognize the politically-established park boundary. Some of man's activities on surrounding national forest, state and private lands, though politically apart from Yellowstone, pose severe threats to the wildlife, water, air, thermal features and other aspects of the park itself.

Nearly every species of plant the earliest explorers might have seen is still to be found in Yellowstone Park. These wildflowers are flourishing near a thermal area. (Tom Dietrich)

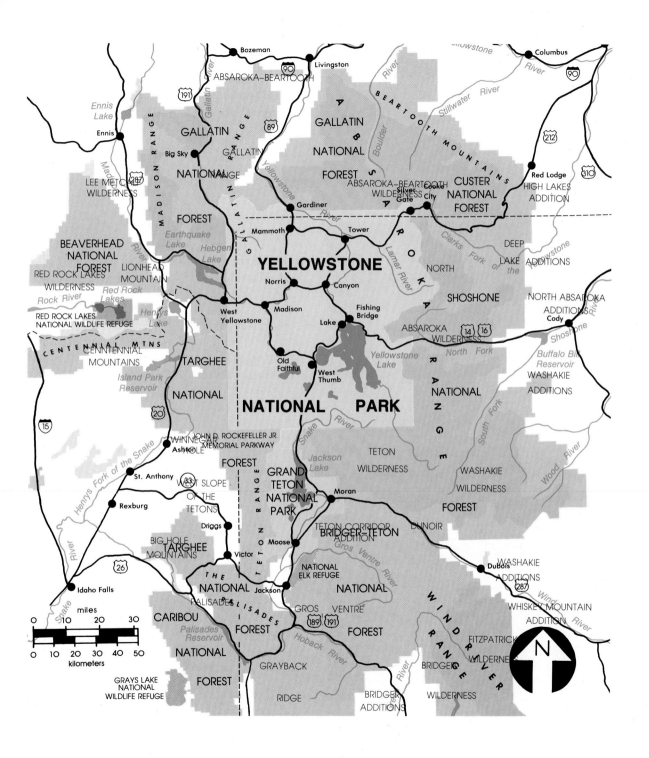

Greater Yellowstone

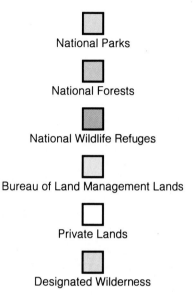

National Parks

National Forests

National Wildlife Refuges

Bureau of Land Management Lands

Private Lands

Designated Wilderness

Bozeman
Livingston
Columbus
90
90
ABSAROKA-BEARTOOTH
191
A
GALLATIN
GALLATIN
BEARTOOTH MOUNTAINS
89
Ennis
Lake
GALLATIN
NATIONAL
212
Big Sky
GALLATIN
RANGE
CUSTER
Red Lodge
287
FOREST
ABSAROKA-BEARTOOTH
NATIONAL
310
Ennis
RANGE
WILDERNESS
B
Cooke
HIGH LAKES
LEE METCALF
FOREST
Silver
City
FOREST
ADDITION
WILDERNESS
Gardiner
Gate
MADISON RANGE
Earthquake
Mammoth
Tower
DEEP
BEAVERHEAD
Lake
S
LAKE
NATIONAL
Hebgen
ADDITIONS
FOREST
Lake
YELLOWSTONE
A
LIONHEAD
R
NORTH
RED ROCK LAKES
MOUNTAIN
Norris
Canyon
O
NORTH ABSAROKA
WILDERNESS
SHOSHONE
ADDITIONS
Rock River
Red Rock
West
Madison
K
Lakes
Yellowstone
Fishing
Cody
RED ROCK LAKES
Henrys
Bridge
A
NATIONAL WILDLIFE REFUGE
Lake
Lake
ABSAROKA
14
16
CENTENNIAL MTNS
WILDERNESS
NATIONAL
Buffalo Bill
CENTENNIAL
Old
Yellowstone
R
Reservoir
MOUNTAINS
Faithful
West
Lake
A
WASHAKIE
TARGHEE
Thumb
N
ADDITIONS
Island Park
G
Reservoir
NATIONAL
E
15
20
NATIONAL
PARK
JOHN D. ROCKEFELLER JR.
WINNEGAR
MEMORIAL PARKWAY
Snake
Ashton
River
FOREST
Jackson
TETON
Lake
WILDERNESS
St. Anthony
33
GRAND
WASHAKIE
TETON
Moran
DUNOIR
Rexburg
WEST SLOPE
NATIONAL
WILDERNESS
OF THE
PARK
TETONS
TETON CORRIDOR
FOREST
Driggs
ADDITION
BRIDGER-TETON
BIG HOLE
Moose
Dubois
TARGHEE
287
MOUNTAINS
Victor
NATIONAL
WASHAKIE
THE
Gros Ventre River
ADDITIONS
Idaho Falls
26
NATIONAL
ELK REFUGE
WHISKEY MOUNTAIN
miles
NATIONAL
ADDITION
Jackson
FOREST
0 10 20 30
PALISADES
GROS
VENTRE
CARIBOU
189 191
FITZPATRICK
0 10 20 30 40 50
Palisades
WILDERNESS
kilometers
Reservoir
NATIONAL
BRIDGER
Hoback River
WINDRIVER
FOREST
GRAYBACK
GRAYS LAKE
RIDGE
BRIDGER
NATIONAL
BRIDGER
WILDERNESS
WILDLIFE REFUGE
ADDITIONS

N

9

Part I

Yellowstone National Park

Bison were reestablished in the park as part of the herculean effort to save the symbol of the west from extinction. It is partly a measure of the park's natural condition that the big beast survives. (Tom Dietrich)

How did it happen that the Yellowstone country was singled out so many years ago for special status as the world's first national park? What made this area of the west so worthy of consideration in the 19th century and so famous in the 20th century?

From the very earliest visitation by white men it was evident that even by comparison to the enormous primeval American wilderness of the early 19th century, Yellowstone was special and in some ways entirely unique. The wonders awaiting the early trappers, prospectors and other explorers who first saw Yellowstone were so incredible, so beyond belief, that when they returned to civilization to report their findings they frequently were regarded as outrageous liars. Their reports of fire, steam, seething earth, enormous waterfalls and petrified forests were so outlandish that the area was for decades discounted as a mythical place. But these men had seen what they said they had: explosive geysers, mud pots, boiling pools, steam vents, cauldrons, sulphur pools, travertine springs and a variety of other phenomena. Had they covered the Yellowstone country entirely they eventually would have encountered more than three hundred geysers and nearly ten thousand other thermal features.

And there was more to the incredible geology of Yellowstone. Though no one could have known it at the time, modern geologists now know that the land across which the early trappers walked has been the site of some of the most massive explosive forces in the discernible geologic history of the planet. One such volcanic eruption left a caldera, a gigantic collapsed crater, some 45 miles wide. Neither could they know of the glaciers, earthquakes or lava flows that have shaped Yellowstone, but we know of them today, and those who take time to learn of them will marvel.

Wednesday, August 31, 1870...Standing there or rather lying there for greater safety, I thought how utterly impossible it would be to describe to another the sensations inspired by such a presence. As I took in this scene, I realized my own littleness, my helplessness, my dread exposure to destruction, my inability to cope with or even comprehend the mighty architecture of nature. More than all this I felt as never before my entire dependence upon that Almighty Power who had wrought these wonders.

NATHANIEL P. LANGFORD

Certainly one of the most famous and most photographed scenes anywhere is the Lower Falls and the so-called Grand Canyon of the Yellowstone River, shown here from Artist Point. (Jeff Gnass)

a

b

c

Nothing can be done well at a speed of forty miles a day....The multitude of mixed, novel impressions rapidly piled on one another make only a dreamy, bewildering, swirling blur, most of which is unrememberable. Far more time should be taken....Climb the mountains and get their good tidings. Nature's peace will flow into you as sunshine flows into trees. The winds will blow their own freshness into you, and the storms their energy, while cares drop off like autumn leaves.

JOHN MUIR, 1898

Many contemporary visitors to Yellowstone confine themselves to roads and automobiles and pass through so quickly they fail to appreciate the real significance of what they are seeing. Were they to spend the time, they would realize that Yellowstone is as unique biologically as it is geologically. The park, in combination with millions of acres of adjoining national forest, comprises what is perhaps the largest and most nearly intact ecosystem remaining in the contiguous United States. Across this region nature still reigns. The heavy imprint of man's interference with naturally functioning biosystems has not yet been felt here.

Yellowstone, the world's first national park, has been designated by the United Nations as a World Heritage Site and an international Biosphere Reserve, recognized for the global value of its thermal features and natural ecosystem.

c

a

b

Opposite page.
(a) Sunset lingers over Norris Geyser Basin. (Fred Hirschmann)
(b) Nearly two and one half million visitors passed through Yellowstone Park in 1983. Many of them never left the confines of their automobiles. (National Park Service)
(c) Cyclists enrolled in the Yellowstone Institute pedal the shore of Yellowstone Lake on a September afternoon. (Rick Reese)
This page.
(a) Crossing the Yellowstone River in the area known as the Thoroughfare Country of southeastern Yellowstone Park. (Wayne Scherr)
(b) Yellowstone Park provides unexcelled opportunities for wildlife photography, but experienced photographers keep a safe distance from their subjects. (Tim Christie)
(c) Fishing instructor Tim Bywater demonstrates fly casting on a section of the Yellowstone River where a "catch and release" policy has been successfully implemented. (Rick Reese)

And Just Beneath the Surface
An Unexploded Natural Bomb

At most places under the earth's crust molten material known as magma is 35 to 40 kilometers down; in some places beneath the deceptive coolness of Yellowstone it may be as shallow as three kilometers. Yellowstone may well be the hottest spot on earth. During the last two million years this hot fluid rock filled large chambers beneath the Yellowstone plateau. Now partially crystallized and solidified, it is still there and is still very hot. About 600,000 years ago this giant reservoir of molten rock pushed up near the surface, slowly bulging and then cracking the ground. Suddenly an extremely violent explosive eruption occurred in which hundreds of cubic miles of material were blown out. The force of that explosion can only be estimated from geologic evidence we discern today, but it was of such a magnitude that nothing during recorded human history approaches it. It was at least a thousand times more powerful than the explosion that blew the top off Washington's Mount St. Helens in 1980. Airborn material from the blast came down at sites more than a thousand miles away; the enormous ash cloud must have dimmed the sun for months on a global scale.

In the wake of this cataclysmic eruption the roofs of the twin magma chambers, which had vented to the surface, collapsed. The result was an immense caldera that sank several thousand feet into the earth across an area roughly 30 by 45 miles. Subsequently, more magma flowed upward and poured out, this time more quietly, eventually filling the floor of the smoldering caldera.

That was not the first time Yellowstone had exploded and it probably won't be the last. In recent geologic history we have evidence of similar activity 1.2 and 2 million years ago in and around Yellowstone. Today resurgent domes, bulges in the earth's surface, are rising in Yellowstone at an extremely rapid rate, geologically speaking. This high rate of uplift is comparable to that of the active volcanoes of Iceland and Hawaii.

What scientists call convective heat flow, or the amount of heat flowing out of an area, is extremely high throughout Yellowstone—more than 20 times higher than average heat flows elsewhere on the continent. In the upper geyser basin alone the amount of heat given off is 800 times greater than the amount given off by non-thermal areas of comparable size. It is this enormous heat source at very shallow depths beneath Yellowstone Park that accounts for the unique thermal features of the area.

Geothermal activity requires water, a heat source, and some mechanism for transferring heat to the water and allowing it to return to the surface. In Yellowstone all three conditions are met and together provide the world's greatest display of geothermal phenomena. Surface water from rain or snow is carried downward through cracks and faults in the earth where it comes in contact with magma-heated rocks. Most of the major thermal areas of Yellowstone are in proximity to the ring of fracture zones that formed around the rim of the Yellowstone caldera where deep cracks and faults act as passageways for surface water to reach the heat source. In other areas of the park, regional fault systems provide conduits for water. The water, sometimes heated to several hundred degrees Fahrenheit, then rises back to the surface, manifesting itself in a number of different ways depending on temperature, pressure, water chemistry and the nature of the fractures and

Trees killed by encroaching thermal features near Black Sand Springs in the Upper Geyser Basin. (Fred Hirschmann)

conduits through which it flows. In Yellowstone the water emerges in powerful geysers, hot springs, steam fumaroles, mud pots and in beautiful terraces from mineral-laden springs.

The thermal features of Yellowstone are unique—there is no parallel to their number and variety anywhere on earth. They are irreplaceable natural features. From experience in other areas of the world we know that such thermal features, especially geysers, are easily disturbed by geothermal exploration and production. Today Yellowstone is probably the only major undisturbed geyser field remaining on earth.

When I arose in the morning [May 20], clouds of vapor seemed like a dense fog to overhang the springs, from which frequent reports or explosions of different loudness, constantly assailed our ears.

WARREN ANGUS FERRIS, 1834

Mud pots at Pocket Basin. (Jeff Gnass photos)

Life in the Hot Pools

In a place such as Yellowstone where man has left nature largely unmolested, we stand to learn some of our greatest lessons. A case in point is the scientific findings that are emerging from our investigations of the life forms inhabiting the thermal environments of the park.

The vivid colors found in many of Yellowstone's thermal waters are caused by living organisms called "thermophilic life." Many of these organisms, both plant and animal, are so perfectly adapted to their special thermal environments that they are found no place else.

Some bacteria can actually live in the boiling water of Yellowstone's thermal features. At temperatures below boiling, vast numbers of other micro-organisms flourish. The greatest number of microbes, both bacteria and algae, live in water between 122 and 140 degrees Fahrenheit. In the more moderate temperatures of hot-spring channels, some animal life is found. Ephydrid flies, for example, can survive continuously up to 109 degrees Fahrenheit feeding on the algae and bacteria of the thermal waters. Another fly, the dolichopodid, is a carnivorous predator that eats the eggs and larvae of ephydrid flies. Life in the form of algae, bacteria and some ephydrid flies even survives in acid springs.

The life forms in such unusual environments may hold valuable secrets for man. These natural organisms may unlock new knowledge about life and its origin or may lead us to profoundly beneficial biological applications as in the case of the recently discovered Sulfolobus acidocaldarius, a

A rarely seen hot spring at the bottom of the Grand Canyon of the Yellowstone. (Fred Hirschmann)

bacteria that obtains its energy by oxidizing sulfur. This organism, which thrives in a hot, acid environment and consumes sulfur, now helps man burn coal more cleanly. We can only speculate about the other secrets held by the life forms of Yellowstone's hot pools.

Opposite page.
(a) Castle Geyser in Yellowstone's Upper Geyser Basin. (Jeff Gnass)
(b) Vivid colors in this runoff channel in the Midway Geyser Basin caused by living plant and animal organisms. (Alice Bengeyfield)
(c) Thermal waters at Norris Geyser Basin. (John Reddy)

... the greatest [scientific] laboratory that nature furnishes on the face of the globe.

FERDINAND V. HAYDEN, 1871 EXPEDITION

17

In the adjacent mountains, beneath the living trees the edges of petrified forests are exposed to view, like specimens on the shelves of a museum, standing on ledges tier above tier where they grew, solemnly silent in rigid crystalline beauty after swaying in the winds thousands of centuries ago, opening marvelous views back into the years and climates and life of the past.

JOHN MUIR, 1898

Right: Petrified trees on Specimen Ridge. (Peter and Alice Bengeyfield)
Opposite page: The Hoodoo Rocks above Mammoth Hot Springs, and Bunsen Peak (background), a long dormant volcano. (Jeff Gnass)

The volcanism that has so violently altered the face of Yellowstone in recent geologic times represents only the latest episode of a very long volcanic history in the area. Some 50 million years ago a number of large volcanoes erupted in the vicinity of Yellowstone Park. Many of these volcanoes were not the violent exploding type, but rather poured out vast quantities of lava and other material in giant flows, which covered several thousand square miles to depths of many thousands of feet. This material comprises much of the Absaroka Range, which forms the northern and eastern portions of present-day Yellowstone National Park.

Intermittently these volcanoes coughed out vast clouds of hot ash, dust, steam, red hot lava and rock fragments that buried everything in their path. It must have been much like the burial of the landscape around Mount St. Helens in 1980, but on a much larger scale. The sudden onset of so much volcanic material under just the right set of conditions buried trees and other plants under a blanket of ash and debris. Mineral-bearing waters flowing through the debris transformed buried plant material into fossils and petrified wood. In order for this to occur, burial had to be rapid enough to prevent decay and gentle enough not to destroy the fragile trees and plants. Water in the right quantities and of the proper chemical composition and temperature also was required. In Yellowstone the conditions were just right to produce one of the most extensive petrified forests on earth.

The petrified forests of Yellowstone include many trees in an upright position, a rarity on such a vast scale. One geological interpretation of these forests is that they occur in layers, perhaps 27 in all, possibly indicating repeated cycles of forest growth, volcanic burial, more forest growth, more burial, and so on. Most unusual indeed! And because of the protection afforded by the creation of Yellowstone National Park 111 years ago, the petrified forests of Yellowstone have been spared most of the vandalism and senseless destruction that have befallen similar features elsewhere in the world. Today these remarkable stone trees are there for all to see, reminders of the dramatic change that has come to the face of this landscape through the eons of time.

18

Yellowstone Park, The World Heritage Site

What does Yellowstone have in common with Australia's Great Barrier Reef, Equador's Galapagos Islands, Egypt's pyramids, Nepal's Katmandu Valley, Tanzania's Serengeti, the historic center of Rome, Auschwitz Concentration Camp, and the Palace of Versailles? The answer: All are areas of such extraordinary natural or cultural significance that they, along with more than a hundred other places, have been designated World Heritage Sites by the UNESCO World Heritage Committee of the United Nations.

Some 53 nations participate in this program, which is intended to identify and protect those natural and cultural areas of the earth that are of outstanding universal value to all the peoples of the world—areas whose loss or diminution would be felt by all who share a common human history and a limited living space on our fragile planet.

In 1978, the U.N. World Heritage Committee initiated Yellowstone National Park into membership in the exclusive club of world heritage sites. Yellowstone was the first American natural area selected.

Reminiscent of a Japanese garden, this is Jupiter Terrace at Mammoth Hot Springs. (Fred Hirschmann)

Yellowstone Park, The World Biosphere Reserve

In 1971, the United Nations Educational, Social and Cultural Organization (UNESCO) acting in a time of what it perceived to be urgent need, embarked upon a program to identify, recognize and promote the conservation of outstanding representative examples of the world's major ecosystems and their components. The project, under the auspices of UNESCO's Man and the Biosphere Program, was an attempt to conserve the dwindling genetic material of the earth's life forms in order to provide a future of maximum global genetic diversity.

It is indicative of its great geological and biological significance that in 1972, Yellowstone was the first area in America to be designated a biosphere reserve. There are now 209 biosphere reserves in 55 countries around the world. "Conserving the Unknown" UNESCO calls it —unknown because when such areas are destroyed we don't know what we're losing in species and in the information they hold; unknown because we don't know what our future perceptions will be of what is a pleasant and livable world.

Those are questions of global concern that go far beyond America's borders.

Morning mist rising from the Grand Canyon of the Yellowstone. (Fred Hirschmann)

Natural management means letting nature do the balancing act between population and available habitat. At right are Rocky Mountain Bighorn Sheep, whose numbers have been reduced by a recent pink eye epidemic. It is difficult for us to understand that healthy looking animals such as the cow elk, far right, may die from the stress imposed by winter. (Michael Francis, Fred Hirschmann)

Letting Nature Take Its Course
Managing Yellowstone as a Natural Area

Though it was primarily the geologic and thermal features of Yellowstone that caught the interest of man and that was largely responsible for the creation of the national park, in more recent times the fabulously abundant and diverse wildlife of the area also has captured the visitor's attention. On a knoll in the Lamar Valley of northeastern Yellowstone, for example, a small group of Yellowstone Institute participants gathered one June evening in 1981 to observe wildlife. In little more than an hour from one location the group spotted elk, moose, mule deer, pronghorn antelope, bison, bighorn sheep, black bears and grizzlies. It may be the only place on the face of the planet where this could be done, for where else does such a variety of animals share a common home except in this one valley of Yellowstone?

In the act of Congress that created Yellowstone National Park on March 1, 1872, it was specified that the area be dedicated and set apart "for the preservation, from injury or despoliation, of all timber, mineral deposits, natural curiosities, or wonders ... and their retention in their natural condition." In modern times the National Park Service has taken seriously its mission of managing Yellowstone as a natural area. It has not always been this way, and some bad mistakes have been made in the past. Today enlightened park managers prefer a continually evolving policy of non-interference with the park's life forms and their natural environment. In practice this means allowing the predator-prey relationship to operate free of interference; allowing the natural forces of winter kill and the carrying capacity of the range to control wildlife numbers; allowing naturally caused fires to burn; avoiding the use of herbicides or pesticides to manipulate the environment and routing humans away from sensitive wildlife areas.

But allowing nature to take its course in Yellowstone is not quite as simple as it may sound, for even though the overwhelming majority of Yellowstone is still wild, the park is not pristine. More than two and one half million people passed through Yellowstone in 1981 and within the park itself there are several major developments including hotels, cabins, restaurants, marinas, campgrounds, curio shops and service stations to accommodate and feed thousands of park visitors and employees every day. Amazingly, park developments including roads, power lines and sewage systems occupy less than one percent of the total park acreage, but man's presence is felt far beyond those areas.

Yellowstone is not entirely pristine in other ways. The natural role of fire was suppressed for many decades in Yellowstone, giving rise to altered forest and plant communities in some areas of the park. Exotic plant species such as timothy and Canadian thistle are widespread and many other exotics occur locally in a variety of locations, especially along the roadside and in areas such as the Lamar Valley, which was under cultivation during the days of the bison ranching there.

The policy of non-interference should not be confused with the policy of no management. Regulations that keep man from disturbing nesting pelicans are "management;" so is the vigorous denial of human garbage to bears, or the closing of grizzly-inhabited trails to hikers.

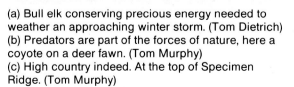

(a) Bull elk conserving precious energy needed to weather an approaching winter storm. (Tom Dietrich)
(b) Predators are part of the forces of nature, here a coyote on a deer fawn. (Tom Murphy)
(c) High country indeed. At the top of Specimen Ridge. (Tom Murphy)

This is the coolest and highest of the parks.

JOHN MUIR, 1898

On Yellowstone Lake. (Fred Hirschmann)

... a vast sheet of quiet water, of a most delicate ultramarine hue, one of the most beautiful scenes I have ever beheld.

FERDINAND V. HAYDEN, 1871 EXPEDITION

Cutthroat trout. (Tom Murphy)

A large number of cutthroat trout in Yellowstone Lake are naturally infested with fish tapeworms and were so long before the arrival of white man. The tapeworms are ugly little devils that crawl out of the fish flesh and across the frying pan when cooking up the morning catch. At another time and in a different place, man might have attempted to eradicate the tapeworm as a "bad" organism parasitic on "good" fish. Under the non-interference policy of Yellowstone, however, the tapeworm is allowed to fulfill its biological role.

We've had a chance in Yellowstone to observe the life cycle of a tapeworm and have discovered some fascinating connections. The adult lives in the digestive tract of Yellowstone Lake birds such as pelicans, gulls, osprey and others. The eggs of the tapeworm are carried in the droppings of these birds, most of which end up in the lake where they are eaten by small fresh-water shrimp; the shrimp in turn are eaten by fish where the tapeworm lodges itself in the flesh. To complete the cycle, the birds, at the top of the food chain, eat the fish. What role the tapeworm plays in its hosts is not known, but it is a natural phenomenon that is allowed to function without interference by man. And so it is with nearly everything in Yellowstone.

In the past non-interference with nature has not always been practiced in Yellowstone. This frequently has yielded colossal blunders, such as the war on predators described in the accompanying story on wolves. At other times interference with nature has had results that, today at least, seem desirable. One such episode lasting more than half a century occurred with the feeding and full-scale ranching of bison. But that interference with nature was undertaken in the name of restoring a creature that had been nearly eliminated by an earlier misdeed of man.

Another example of management interference to correct the results of earlier actions by man can be seen in the highly controversial Yellowstone bear policy. For 80 years bears in Yellowstone had feasted on human garbage, and it had become the major food source for many park bears. Several large open-dump sites in and immediately adjacent to the park became congregating locations, especially for grizzlies. On one night in 1966 for example, 88 grizzlies were observed at the Trout Creek dump. Park bears also were obtaining human food from other sources: anywhere there were garbage cans, in campers' coolers, and along the roadside, where eager visitors fed begging black bears.

In 1967, the National Park Service began a policy of denying garbage and other human food to bears. By the fall of 1970 the park's open-pit garbage dumps were closed; by 1971 garbage cans were bear-proofed and rules regulating food storage in campgrounds were implemented. This was a management decision to interfere with long established, but nevertheless unnatural, feeding habits of the bear. The policy caused a storm of controversy and was opposed vigorously by bear researchers John and Frank Craighead who argued that sudden denial of garbage would have disastrous consequences on the Yellowstone grizzly population. Now 15 years

Truly symbolic of the problems of natural management in a confined and perhaps shrinking ecosystem is the grizzly bear. (Alan Carey)

This page.
(a) Mule deer buck. (Alan Carey)
(b) Canada geese. (Alan Carey)
(c) Young great horned owl. (Tim Christie)
(d) Black bear. (Tim Christie)

Opposite page.
(a) Yellow-rumped warbler. (Ron Shade)
(b) Blue grouse. (Tim Christie)
(c) Snowshoe hare. (Ron Shade)
(d) Pine marten. (Tom Murphy)
(e) Pronghorn fawns. (Ron Shade)

a

b

c

d

e

later, the jury is still out on the dump controversy, but for whatever reason, there appears to have been a reduction in the number of Yellowstone grizzlies; some would say to a point where they may not be able to recover.

In response to declining grizzly populations, some persons are proposing that supplemental feeding of grizzly bears in Yellowstone may be necessary during periods of critical natural food shortages. Many bear biologists oppose supplemental feeding and share the concern expressed by Chris Servheen, grizzly-bear specialist for the U.S. Fish and Wildlife Service, when he asks, "Do we want grizzly bears if the only way to have them is to feed them in a big pile?" But right or wrong a deliberate manipulation of the natural ecosystem at least is being proposed as one way to restore a healthy bear population. So while the official management policy for Yellowstone National Park today is to let nature take its course without interference from man, in some cases (such as the elimination of wolves, the denial of historic winter range, or the garbage-hooked bears) man has so altered natural systems that he must re-interfere to try to restore them. It remains to be seen if this can ever be fully achieved, but if it can, it's likely that Yellowstone is where it will happen.

Greater Yellowstone is large enough, remote enough, diverse enough, and, with the exception of wildlife poaching, protected enough to provide most, and in some cases all, of the necessary ingredients for a smooth-functioning, self-regulating ecosystem. Presumably if man pulled out of the area today, totally absenting himself from five or six million acres, native plant and animal life forms would continue to survive, even flourish. That is so because sufficient area remains in a natural condition for self-sustaining, self-balancing natural forces to function. This isn't true of most areas in America today—man has so interfered with his environment that he is now compelled to hold it together by ever more artificial means: by building dams to control floods caused by our destruction of watershed; by using pesticides to control insects which are out of control because we have destroyed the creatures that prey on them; by poisoning coyotes because they are eating sheep because we have poisoned the rodents which were the coyote's primary food source, and so on.

That natural systems continue to function fairly well in Greater Yellowstone in the 1980s is no accident. Historically Yellowstone Park itself has been protected by its national park status against a host of threats. Much of the rest of Greater Yellowstone has been afforded some political protection in forest reserves, national wildlife refuges and in Grand Teton National Park. Topography, climate and remoteness also have played some role in protecting the area.

In the last several decades, however, much of Greater Yellowstone has come under commodity-producing pressures, notably from large-scale timber and mineral development and sharply increasing numbers of people. Until very recently, the plant and animal life of the park was still relatively secure because habitats were secure, but as pressures on surrounding lands intensify the effect is being felt deep inside Yellowstone.

Portions of Yellowstone Park are covered with vegetation to support up to 25,000 elk on various summer ranges. But this is high country, and heavy snows blanket it for more than half the year. Thus, the real carrying capacity of the land is determined by its scarce winter range. Some of it lies beyond the park boundary on surrounding national forest and private lands. This winter range is essential to the Yellowstone elk herds, but it is beyond the geographical and in most cases the political control of National Park Service managers. The same thing can be said to a lesser extent

(a) New-born elk calf. (Tom Murphy)
(b) Handsome example of big horn sheep. (Peter and Alice Bengeyfield)
(c) Salad days for the moose. (Peter and Alice Bengeyfield)

Slough Creek and Cutoff Mountain just inside the northern boundary of Yellowstone Park. (Tom Murphy)

We stopped at this place and for my own part I almost wished I could spend the remainder of my days in a place like this where happiness and contentment seemed to reign in wild romantic splendor surrounded by majestic battlements which seemed to support the heavens and shut out all hostile intruders.

OSBORNE RUSSELL, 1835 in JOURNAL OF A TRAPPER

for others of Yellowstone's wildlife species. Grizzly bears range widely beyond the park, mule deer and bighorn sheep cross freely back and forth across park boundaries, bald eagles, trumpeter swans and pelicans cover hundreds, sometimes thousands, of miles outside the park each year. Yellowstone Park itself simply is not large enough to provide all that her creatures require.

Commercial logging and, with a few small exceptions, domestic livestock grazing have never been permitted in Yellowstone Park. As a result plant communities here present us with a relatively good picture of the natural processes of plant succession. As in the case of Yellowstone's wildlife, man's interference with plant life has been felt to a degree through such practices as fire suppression, some limited farming, a pesticide attack on insects and a few other intrusions, but plant life in most of Yellowstone today is probably as natural as any to be found. There are about 1,000 species of flowering plants and 13 species of trees in the park, not a particularly diverse plant community, but not surprising in light of the history of recent volcanism and glaciation and the high elevations. Eighty percent of Yellowstone is forested. Of the trees found in the park eight are coniferous, and of those the lodgepole pine is by far the most common.

The special relationship between fire and the lodgepole pine is yet another of the remarkable natural dramas that we can observe in Yellowstone. The lodgepole thrives in post-fire environments and many have what are called serotinous cones, which release seeds in the heat of a fire to regenerate new forests. Other species occur only in post-fire environments where increased sunlight and reduced competition for nutrients contribute to the growth of shrubs, wildflowers, berries and vigorous stands of new trees. Many animals and birds also do well in burned-over areas,

Left: Lightning strikes a high ridge in the North Absaroka Wilderness area along Yellowstone's eastern boundary. (Fred Hirschmann)
Below: Fire sweeps through the forest on the southwest side of Jackson Lake in Grand Teton National Park. In this case the fire was viewed as one of nature's management tools and was allowed to burn, eventually consuming about 2,000 acres of old lodgepole pine forest. (Rick Reese)

as new sources of forage and nesting sites for birds are provided.

For many years, man attempted to suppress natural lightning-caused fires in western forests, and Yellowstone was no exception. With the advent of fire patrols by aircraft in the 1950s, fire suppression became far more effective. For a period of about 20 years fire was not allowed to play its role as a thinning agent in Yellowstone. It is estimated that about 10 percent of all the park's lodgepole was affected. During the past decade the National Park Service has adopted a "let-burn

policy" for lightning caused fires that do not threaten man or property in the park. Many fires have been allowed to run their course under this policy and in most instances fire is once again playing its role in Yellowstone's forests.

There is something else going on in Yellowstone's forests that man once tried to interfere with but has now learned to let run its natural course: insect infestations. In recent years tens of thousands of Yellowstone lodgepoles have been killed by an infestation of mountain pine beetles, which bore into trees and so

a

b

c

d

e

f

(a) A bird's-eye view of a lodgepole pine forest shows how insects attack selectively, killing primarily the older mature trees and ignoring younger healthy ones. (Wayne Scherr)

(b) Fire in this lodgepole forest has increased the amount of sunlight reaching the forest floor and reduced competition for nutrients, allowing a diverse new growth of shrubs, flowers, berries and young trees to emerge. (Rick Graetz)

(c) Clematis. (Tom Murphy)

(d) Columbine. (Tom Murphy)

(e) Fringed gentian. (Tom Murphy)

(f) As young lodgepole pine stands grow, they cast shade on the forest floor, and the quantity and diversity of understory vegetation diminishes. (Fred Hirschmann)

diminish their flow of resin that they die. For several years park managers fought the beetle infestation in an effort to save the forests. The battle was eventually abandoned, perhaps as much for its futility as for the emerging recognition that the beetle epidemics were a natural phenomenon that played a positive role in the complex scheme of energy exchanges occurring in the forest. To the casual observer, a forest under attack by the beetle may appear to be annihilated, but this is not so. In fact, the beetle infestation is highly selective, affecting primarily older, mature trees and ignoring the younger ones. The inner bark of young, healthy trees is too thin for beetles to survive.

The beetles come and go in cycles that are dependent upon favorable weather conditions and food supply. They are, along with fire, nature's way of thinning the forest and allowing younger trees to flourish. Beetle-killed trees are not wasted. Their snags provide perching and nesting sites for hawks and eagles and for cavity-nesting birds such as the mountain bluebird. The forest floor is transformed, ground nesting birds find protected nest sites and other forms of wildlife find greater cover and feeding opportunities. Many of the birds that benefit from the altered forest prey on beetles; browse, berries and forage appear where none was found before. The self-regulating capacity of nature's way has worked its magic.

In a myriad of ways similar mechanisms are at work in Yellowstone's spruce-fir forest, alpine tundra, marshland, sagebrush-grassland and aquatic plant communities. In Yellowstone where the heavy imprint of man's interference has not yet been felt, we can still see the functioning of these natural marvels and develop an appreciation for the interrelatedness of the natural world and of our very modest place in it as just one among God's creatures.

a

b

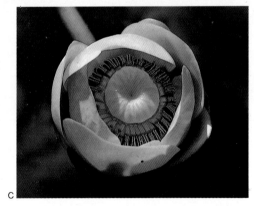
c

This page.
(a) The headwaters of the Yellowstone River meander toward Yellowstone Lake. (Tom Murphy)
(b) Lily pond. (Peter and Alice Bengeyfield)
(c) Flower of the water lily. (Tom Murphy)

Opposite page.
(a) Union Falls near the south boundary of Yellowstone National Park. (Fred Hirschmann)
(b) Dew-coated spider web on a lodgepole pine (Fred Hirschmann)

To this place it comes from a deep gorge in the mountains enters a valley lying Nth & South about 15 Ms. long and 3 wide thro. which it winds its way slowly to the Nth. thro swamps and marshes and calmly reposes in the bosom of the Yellow Stone Lake. The South extremity of this valley is smooth and thickly clothed with high meadow grass surrounded by high craggy mountains topped with snow.

OSBORNE RUSSELL, 1836
in JOURNAL OF A TRAPPER

a

b

c

a. Sedge Creek along Yellowstone Lake. (Jeff Gnass)
b. Doane and Stevenson Peaks. (Michael Francis)
c. Bridge Bay Marina, YNP. (Tom Dietrich)

"A thousand Yellowstone wonders are calling, 'Look up and down and round about you!'"

John Muir, 1898
West Yellowstone

35

Beyond Yellowstone Park: Greater Yellowstone Defined

Looking south across Yellowstone Park toward the Teton Range, some 75 miles distant. (Mike and Barb Pflaum)

Certainly it is the largest relatively intact ecosystem remaining in the lower 48 states, but it is tiny when compared to the rest of the nation. You can drive through the area in almost any direction in a few hours. It is the largest, but it is not large.

FRANZ CAMENZIND
WYOMING BIOLOGIST

The vastness of Yellowstone National Park is deceiving, for though it covers some 3,500 square miles, it is not large enough to survive independently and apart from its biological, ecological and geological context. As we already have noted the park is not an island, and nature does not recognize the lines we have drawn on the map and call park boundaries.

In some very important respects, activities on the lands surrounding Yellowstone National Park pose severe threats to wildlife, thermal features, air, water and other aspects of Yellowstone itself. The environmental integrity of the park depends on careful management of these lands, most of which must remain in an essentially natural condition to protect Yellowstone.

The boundaries that Congress created for Yellowstone National Park were drawn to include the thermal features of the area and Yellowstone Lake, but largely ignored biological considerations. We have learned much since that time. When Congress enacted the Alaska National Interest Lands Conservation Act in 1980, emphasis was placed on trying to draw park and wildlife refuge boundaries to include entire ecosystems. Yellowstone's boundaries were drawn in 1872 as a simple giant rectangle approximately 62 by 54 miles, containing well over 2 million acres. The concepts of watershed, wildlife migration routes, biological communities and intact ecosystems were not known at that time. Geology more than biology was the main criterion for the establishment of the park boundary.

It didn't take long, however, for some observers to recognize that Yellowstone's boundaries did not make much sense on the ground. General Philip H. Sheridan, the Civil War hero who visited Yellowstone in 1882, suggested then that the size of the park be vastly increased to extend beyond the exist-

To be sure, the emphasis on logging to the exclusion of wildlife, recreation and other values is nothing new in the Forest Service, an agency that employs nearly 6,000 foresters and only 523 wildlife biologists, and the increased intensity of timber cutting on our national forest will not abate in the near future if the statements of John Crowell, Assistant Secretary of Agriculture in charge of the Forest Service, are any indication. Crowell says he wants the Forest Service to double the timber cut on our national forests between now and the end of the century.

In the Greater Yellowstone Ecosystem logging is of concern in several areas. Foremost among these is the Targhee National Forest which completely surrounds the southwest corner of Yellowstone National Park. (See satellite photo on this page.) The largest timber sale ever made outside Alaska was made here on the Moose Creek Plateau adjacent to Yellowstone. The sale totalled 318 million board feet of timber, and when the last tree falls more than a hundred square miles of the area will have been cut. Forest Service officials explain that much of the lodgepole pine on the Targhee near Yellowstone has been attacked by the pine beetle and is dead or dying and therefore needs to be cut now to salvage it from loss. In the four years between 1974 and 1978, the cut on the Targhee tripled.

The policy of accelerated cutting on the Targhee on the basis of beetle infestation may mean that other resource values, notably wildlife, are being sacrificed. A recently released Targhee National Forest Plan states that for the areas adjacent to Yellowstone on the west: "A heavy short-term impact on wildlife habitat and visual resources will occur in order to accelerate salvage and regeneration of lodgepole pine stands killed by the mountain pine beetle." The plan notes that logging will affect 7,200 acres of Situation I grizzly bear habitat each year.

ERTS/LANDSAT satellite image of Yellowstone Park and surrounds. (Courtesy of EROS Data Center, U.S. Geological Survey)

I don't consider Yellowstone Park as an island that can be self-perpetuated...All these activities in combination become a tremendous threat to Yellowstone.

JOHN TOWNSLEY
SUPERINTENDENT OF YELLOWSTONE NATIONAL PARK, 1975—1982

Large logging clear cuts on the Gallatin National Forest along Yellowstone's western boundary. The town of West Yellowstone, Montana can be seen near the center of the photo. (Rick Graetz)

At some future time, if we desire to do so, we can repeal the law [creating Yellowstone National Park] if it is in somebody's way.

SEN. LYMAN TRUMBALL, SPEAKING ABOUT LEGISLATION FOR THE CREATION OF YELLOWSTONE NATIONAL PARK, 1872

ing boundaries 40 miles to the east and 10 miles to the south in order to encompass a more cohesive wildlife reserve. Though Sheridan's suggestion was never acted upon, there was considerable discussion about expanding the park boundary during the next 50 years. In 1917, Secretary of the Interior Franklin Lane recommended a large addition to Yellowstone that would have encompassed the Teton Mountain Range, Jackson Hole and much of what we know today as the Teton Wilderness. Lane's proposal would have added 1,200 square miles to Yellowstone National Park, and it came very close to receiving congressional approval.

In the meantime several presidents empowered by the Forest Reserve Act of 1891 had created large forest reserves on land east and south of Yellowstone. In 1891, President Harrison signed an order creating a "public forest reservation" known as the Yellowstone National Park Timberland Reserve along all of the east and a portion of the south park boundary. In 1897 President Cleveland set aside the Teton Forest Reserve, encompassing much of the Jackson Hole country. In 1902 both areas were expanded significantly by President Theodore Roosevelt. Almost all of these lands have since become part of the national forest system or have been integrated into Grand Teton National Park.

Though General Sheridan early recognized that the boundaries of Yellowstone Park didn't correspond to the distribution of its wildlife populations, it probably didn't make much difference in 1882. The law creating Yellowstone did little to protect the wildlife or natural features of the park, and at the time of Sheridan's visit, wildlife inside Yellowstone was managed essentially the same as it was outside. More importantly, most of the country around Yellowstone at that time remained in a natural condition, not because anyone was protecting it, but because there were few

demands to exploit or develop the area. Where there was a marketable resource, it was difficult and expensive to extract. But in recent years these demands have escalated dramatically to a point where they are now affecting or threatening to affect such large and sensitive areas that we are compelled to acknowledge that Yellowstone Park's living systems and thermal features may not survive intact unless large areas of land surrounding it are managed with priority given to the needs of the park.

Those concerned about the threats to Yellowstone from activities on adjacent federal, state and private lands would, of course, dearly love to re-draw the boundaries of the park to include within it those nearby areas upon which the environmental integrity of Yellowstone depends. Others more interested in logging, mining, oil and gas and geothermal exploration and production, roads, dams, recreational and second-home developments and a myriad of other interests doubtless also would like to re-draw Yellowstone's boundaries. But it is unlikely that the boundaries of Yellowstone National Park will change much. Some adjustments and additions to park lands, however, could occur as threats to the park become more imminent.

Taking the current ownership and administrative authority over these lands as a given, we must focus our attention on a management of Greater Yellowstone as a region of concern, a biological community, an ecosystem, a geological thermal system, and whatever else we might wish to call it, as long as we recognize that Yellowstone National Park is not an island, cut off and unrelated to adjacent lands. It is, rather, part of a much larger and highly interrelated "Greater Yellowstone" area.

How we define the geographic extent of Greater Yellowstone depends upon which of its characteristics we use as criteria for delin-

The northern border of the Greater Yellowstone Ecosystem is formed by the Absaroka-Beartooth Wilderness Area. This is the Twin Lakes area. (Wayne Scherr)

eating boundaries. Were wildlife biologists to employ their criteria, they might take into account the entire community of wildlife centered in Yellowstone but ranging far beyond park boundaries. By this measure, an ecosystem includes all of the elements required to perpetuate all of the species indigenous to an area including a substantial amount of genetic exchange between populations of major vertebrates. It would also include the winter ranges for migrating mammals, which in some instances lie at considerable distances from the park itself but which are essential for the survival of healthy wildlife populations. It also might include the range for natural diffusion (as opposed to seasonal migration) from one part of the biological community to another. To a wildlife biologist, the outer boundaries of Greater Yellowstone could therefore be drawn at barriers to migration or diffusion. Such barriers might be man-made and includes areas of concentrated human settlement, highways, major mining or logging operations, dams and reservoirs, or agricultural developments.

Geologists, on the other hand, might define Greater Yellowstone in terms of major geological formations or landforms, or might include large areas of geothermal resources that lie outside Yellowstone to the north, west and southwest. These boundaries would differ substantially from the rectangle that Congress established in 1872.

A third approach to defining Greater Yellowstone could employ hydrographic criteria and focus on Greater Yellowstone as an area that encompasses the headwaters of the rivers and streams that arise on the high bubble of earth known as the Yellowstone Plateau.

Right: Black Peak in the Gros Ventre Mountains southeast of Jackson Hole, Wyoming. (U.S. Forest Service)
Above: August wildflowers in the Wyoming portion of the Beartooth Range near the northeastern boundary of Yellowstone Park. (Jeff Gnass)

Dusk in Montana's Paradise Valley north of Yellowstone Park. (John Reddy)

... conservation areas do not act as true islands in a barren ocean, but interact with their surrounding region.

UNESCO, MAN AND THE BIOSPHERE PROGRAMME

The first fall on the Yellowstone, Hawkins and myself were coming up the river in search of camp, when we discovered a very large bar on the opposite bank. We shot across, and thought we had killed him, fur he laid quite still. ...we tied our mules and left our guns, clothes, and everything except our knives and belts, and swum over to whar the bar war. But instead of being dead, as we expected, he sprung up as we come near him, and took after us. Then you ought to have seen two naked men run! It war a race for life, and a close one, too. But we made the river first. The bank war about fifteen feet high above the water, and the river ten or twelve feet deep; but we didn't halt. Overboard we went, the bar after us.... You can reckon that I swam! Every moment I felt myself being washed into the yawning jaws of the mighty beast, whose head war up the stream, and his eyes on me. But the current war too strong for him, and swept him along as fast as it did me....Hawkins war the first to make the shore, unknown to be bar, whose head war still up stream; and he set up such a whooping and yelling that the bar landed too, but on the opposite side. I made haste to follow Hawkins, who had landed on the side of the river we started from, either by design or good luck: and then we traveled back a mile and more to whar our mules war left...

JOE MEEK, as told to FRANCES VICTOR
in THE RIVER OF THE WEST, 1870

A fall morning on the Lewis River. (Jeff Gnass)

This high country in and immediately adjacent to Yellowstone National Park gives rise to every major river and stream within a radius of 100 miles. The Yellowstone, Gallatin and Madison rivers are born here, and the mountains of the park's eastern boundary give rise to the Clark's Fork of the Yellowstone, the Shoshone, and the Grey Bull rivers. All of these rivers flow east from the Continental Divide. It is also within the park proper where the Snake River begins its course west of the Continental Divide, first south into Jackson Hole then generally west to its confluence with the Columbia near Pasco in southeast Washington State.

Immediately west of the park boundary, the Henry's Fork flows south for miles through the Island Park region before dropping sharply off the rim of an ancient caldera into the farmlands of Idaho where it joins the Snake. In the extreme southeastern reaches of this area, just 50 miles from the corner of the park, the Green River begins its long journey southward through Wyoming and Utah to its confluence with the Colorado in the canyonlands of the southwest. Across a high divide just a few miles northwest of the upper Green, the waters of the Gros Ventre River originate and flow off to join the Snake River in the middle of Jackson Hole.

While each of these approaches to defining Greater Yellowstone have merit, none of them alone possesses the precision, comprehensive scope and objectivity we desire. For this reason, we have opted to use the concepts of ecosystem and ecoregion developed by R. G. Bailey and A. W. Kuchler, and adopted by the U.S. Forest Service for use in its Roadless Area Review and Evaluation II (RARE II) studies during the late 1970s. Although a bit more complex than the other approaches described above, the ecosystem concept has the advantage of being based on observable properties and of providing us with boundar-

ies that encompass the wildlife communities and unique geological phenomena of this region.

Bailey and Kuchler describe an ecosystem as "any potential natural vegetation-type within an ecoregion." Potential vegetation is "vegetation that would exist today if man were removed from the scene and if the plant succession after his removal were telescoped into a single moment." (This should not be confused with the actual vegetation observed at the present.)

The map on page 44 shows the area of similar potential natural vegetation in the

The Henry's Fork River flows through Idaho's Harriman State Park west of Yellowstone Park. (Harriman State Park)

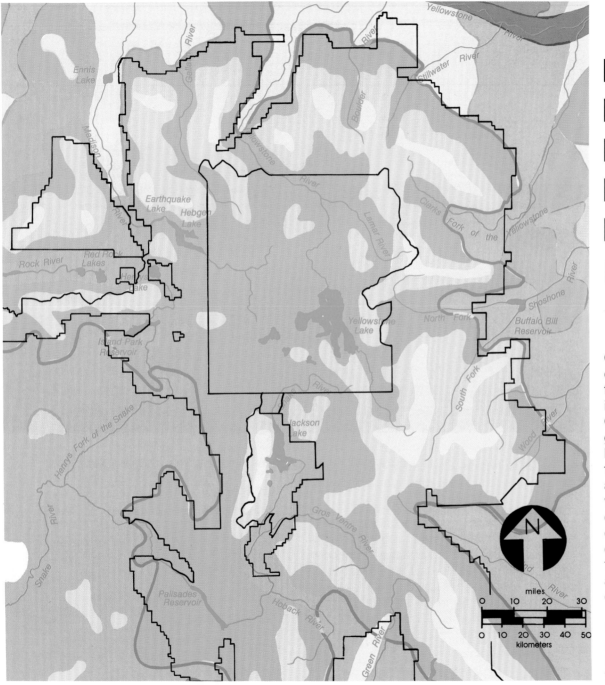

Potential Natural Vegetation

- Alpine Meadows and Barren Ground
- Western Spruce Fir Forest
- Douglas Fir Forest
- Sagebrush Steppe
- Northern Flood Plain Forest
- Wheatgrass — Needle Grass Shrub Steppe/Grama — Needlegrass —Wheatgrass
- Foothills Prairie
- Saltbrush — Greasewood
- Desert: Vegetation Largely Absent
- Eastern Ponderosa Forest
- National Forest and Park Outlines
- Rocky Mountain Forest Province Boundary

● Adapted from A. W. Kuchler and R. G. Baily, Ecosystem of the United States, USDA 1978

Greater Yellowstone area. Bailey's criteria for ecosystem classification according to potential natural vegetation clearly shows that there is an ecological community we can call Greater Yellowstone and that its boundaries generally coincide with boundaries that might be based on wildlife considerations. Wildlife, for example, depends on plants for food, and at times for shelter and breeding areas as well. Even where plants do not control wildlife distribution, they often indicate the kinds of climate and soil types upon which wildlife depends. From this it seems we can in fact talk of the "Greater Yellowstone ecosystem" as a definable ecological entity with fairly well defined boundaries.

The map on page 45 delineates the boundaries of the Greater Yellowstone ecosystem as we will define them in this book. Our map shows an ecosystem somewhat smaller than the area of potential natural vegetation depicted in the map on page 44 because we

The Greater Yellowstone
Ecosystem

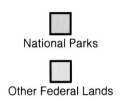

National Parks

Other Federal Lands

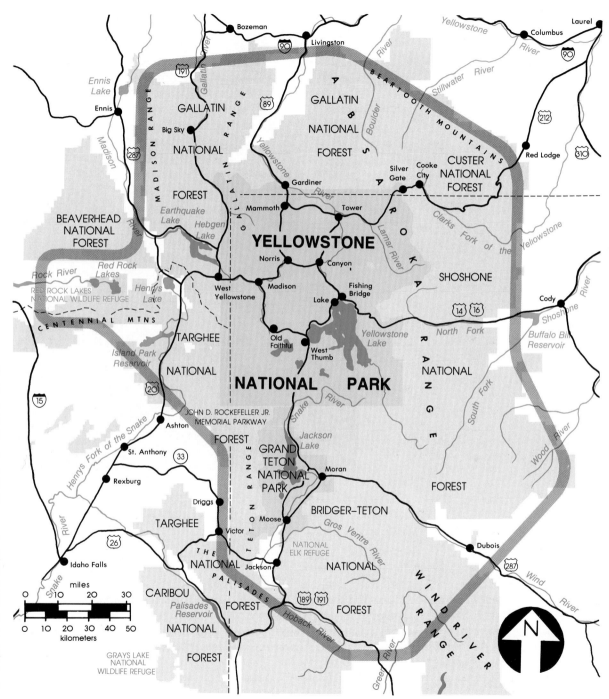

have cut off the long legs which extend to the south and the southeast. These legs, which extend for miles to the south and southeast, were omitted simply because of their distance from the center of the ecosystem. This was not a judgment based on ecological grounds, but rather one made on editorial grounds. These deletions from our definition of the ecosystem are of course arbitrary, and a case certainly could be made for including them.

While the concept of potential natural vegetation provides us with a definition of the Greater Yellowstone ecosystem, one needn't be a scientist to see the connections that tie Yellowstone Park to its surroundings. We said earlier that some of Yellowstone's wildlife species range far beyond the national park boundary and depend heavily on adjacent lands for survival. Two of Yellowstone's most famous inhabitants, the grizzly bear and elk, illustrate this point.

The Grizzly Bear: The Park Is Not Enough

It is estimated that in 1800 there were perhaps 100,000 grizzly bears roaming North America — today there are probably less than 1,000. The great bears in the Yellowstone area are a remnant population, tied to ever-diminishing wild lands. Grizzlies disappeared from Texas in 1890, passed from former abundance to extinction in California in 1922, were gone from Utah by 1923, Oregon by 1931, New Mexico by 1933, and Arizona by 1935. Today, only two areas remain in the entire lower 48 states where significant populations of grizzlies survive. One is the Greater Yellowstone Ecosystem, the other is the area sometimes referred to as the Northern Continental Divide Ecosystem, which includes Glacier National Park and large areas of formally designated wilderness in the Bob Marshall, Great Bear, Scapegoat and Mission Mountain wilderness areas to the south of Glacier, and Canadian wild lands to the north.

Yellowstone National Park is what biologists call a grizzly population center, an area essential to the survival of the bear, and an area where the grizzly's activity under natural, free-ranging conditions is common. Habitat needed for the survival of the species is found here. Not surprisingly, however, the biological boundaries of the Yellowstone grizzly population center don't stop at the national park boundary—indeed, they reach far beyond the lands of the park. By even the most conservative estimates, 1.7 million acres of the population center (referred to by federal agencies as Situation I Management Area) lie outside the park. At the bare minimum, more than 40 percent of the essential habitat of Yellowstone

The grizzly bear—ursus arctos horribillis. His continued existence is at the mercy of man. (Doug O'looney)

Permanent grizzly ranges and permanent wilderness areas are of course two names for one problem. Enthusiasm about either requires a long view of conservation, and a historical perspective. Only those able to see the pageant of evolution can be expected to value its theater, the wilderness, or its outstanding achievement, the grizzly. But if education really educates, there will, in time, be more and more citizens who understand that relics of the old West add meaning and value to the new. Youth yet unborn will pole up the Missouri with Lewis and Clark, or climb the Sierras with James Capen Adams, and each generation in turn will ask: Where is the big white bear? It will be a sorry answer to say he went under while conservationists weren't looking.

ALDO LEOPOLD
A SAND COUNTY ALMANAC, 1948

grizzly bears lies beyond the park, and the distribution of grizzly bears is not limited only to the Situation I population centers. In 1979, the U.S. Fish and Wildlife Service designated **an area within the Greater Yellowstone ecosystem as occupied territory (See map on this page.),** a term that refers to an area in which confirmed grizzly bear sightings have occurred with some frequency in recent years. Yet even the area defined as occupied territory probably understates the distribution of the bear in the Greater Yellowstone area. The boundaries of occupied territory were arrived at through a series of compromises, some made on the basis of political considerations. It is unlikely that it encompasses the entire range of the Yellowstone grizzly, and it should not be construed as a fixed line. Rather it should be seen as a fuzzy line, miles in width and encompassing a considerably larger area.

Under the provisions of the Endangered Species Act of 1973, when a species is listed as threatened or endangered (the grizzly was listed as threatened in 1975), the U.S. Fish and Wildlife Service is supposed to designate critical habitat as a "means whereby the ecosystem upon which endangered species depend, may be considered, protected or restored." The critical habitat proposed by the agency in the mid-'70s was considerably larger than the occupied territory defined in 1979. The Situation I habitat used today is far smaller than either the occupied or the originally proposed critical habitat.

We needn't argue about how far beyond the boundaries of Yellowstone National Park the home of the grizzly bear extends, so long as we recognize that it extends far beyond — encompassing a total area at least twice the size of the park itself. "It is blatantly clear," John Townsley, former superintendent of Yellowstone Park was quoted as saying in 1982, "that the grizzly bear cannot survive if Yellow-

The Greater Yellowstone Occupied Grizzly Bear Habitat

National Parks

Other Federal Lands

stone National Park is its only refuge. It also needs portions of the five adjacent forests." A similar point is made by Dick Knight, leader of the Interagency Grizzly Bear Study Team, a group of bear researchers that has studied the Yellowstone grizzly for 10 years, when he says, "Most grizzly bears cross state, forest and park boundaries several times a year, making populations within any political jurisdiction meaningless, and cooperative management a necessity." Clearly for the bear, as for nearly every other species and ecological relationship, Yellowstone Park is not an island.

But while Yellowstone National Park is not an island for the grizzly bear, the Greater Yel-

lowstone ecosystem is. As the map on this page demonstrates, there is no corridor for bears to move from Greater Yellowstone to another area of suitable bear habitat outside this ecosystem. By contrast, the Glacier Park grizzly is far better able to move long distances over contiguous areas of good habitat throughout the Bob Marshall complex to the south, and to the north far into Canada. But the Yellowstone grizzly is, in essence, trapped in Greater Yellowstone—if it is to live at all, all of its needs, including areas safe from man, **must be met here. There is nowhere else to go.**

Left: A high basin in the Washakie Wilderness near the southeasten corner of Yellowstone Park. (Howie Wolke)
Below: Boy Scout auction of elk antlers collected on the National Elk Refuge, Jackson, Wyoming. Oriental buyers, who value the antlers for their alleged aphrodisiac and medicinal purposes, pay $6 per pound for the antlers. The 1982 antler auction shown here yielded $50,000. (U.S. Forest Service)

About 4,000 elk inhabit the southern reaches of Yellowstone National Park during the summer and fall months. Since this portion of the park does not constitute a complete ecological unit in which the elk can survive year round, the herd migrates south out of the park to lower elevations and suitable winter range. With the destruction of their historic winter range (caused primarily by human settlement and agricultural development), many of the elk now concentrate at the National Elk Refuge in Jackson, Wyoming where they are fed pellets and hay to make it through the winter. Without the refuge or without migration corridors to reach it, some of the southern Yellowstone elk would perish. They too have no place else to go.

In addition to the southern Yellowstone elk herd, other major herds migrate to non-park lands for winter range. (See map page 49.) The park's largest collection of elk, known as the northern Yellowstone elk herd, summers across nearly two-thirds of Yellowstone Park, but moves north into the lower valleys of the Lamar and Yellowstone rivers as winter approaches. During periods of the deepest snowfall, about 15 percent of the northern herd, whose numbers now appear to have stabilized at about 16,000 animals, will migrate down the Yellowstone River out of the park and into Montana where it winters on state, private and national forest lands. In the northwest corner of the park, the Gallatin elk herd travels up to 20 miles into the Gallatin

Canyon of southwestern Montana. And near the southwestern corner of the park a smaller herd of perhaps 300 to 500 elk migrates out of the Bechler River area across the Targhee National Forest of Idaho to winter range on the Sand Creek Desert more than 25 miles beyond the park boundary. Other herds move out of the park to the east and southeast crossing onto the North Absaroka and Washakie wilderness areas and adjacent lands. Such migrations, of course, are not limited to elk; other wildlife species such as pronghorn, deer, bighorn sheep and a variety of birds and fish also move back and forth across national park, national forest, state and private lands in Montana, Wyoming and Idaho.

Seasonal Elk Migration

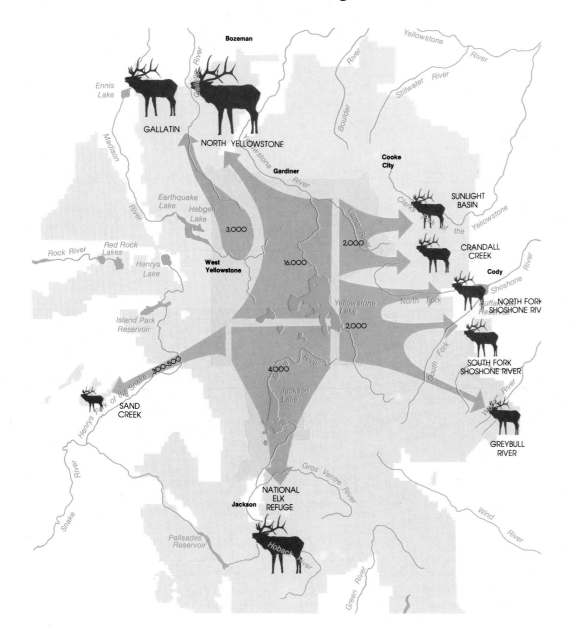

Bozeman

GALLATIN

NORTH YELLOWSTONE

Ennis Lake

Gardiner

Cooke City

Earthquake Lake

Hebgen Lake

3,000

SUNLIGHT BASIN

West Yellowstone

16,000

2,000

CRANDALL CREEK

Cody

Rock River

Red Rock Lakes

Henrys Lake

Island Park Reservoir

Yellowstone Lake

North Fork

NORTH FORK SHOSHONE RIV

2,000

SOUTH FORK SHOSHONE RIVER

300-500

SAND CREEK

4,000

Jackson Lake

GREYBULL RIVER

Snake

NATIONAL ELK REFUGE

Jackson

Gros Ventre River

Wind River

Palisades Reservoir

Green River

Hoback River

EIK lying in grass

Antlers in velvet, a skin-like substance circulating blood and nourishment to the bony growth. (Tom Dietrich)

National Parks   Other Federal Lands

Right: Bull and cow elk in the autumn breeding season. (Tim Christie)

Below: Elk from Yellowstone's northern herd wintering in the Lamar Valley. (Michael Francis)

The true test of the nature of national character is in what people choose, by a conscious act, in the face of contending choices, to preserve.

ROBIN W. WINKS, CHAIRMAN
NATIONAL PARK SERVICE ADVISORY BOARD

Aspen scrabble for an existence in an outcrop of limestone. (Jeff Gnass)

The Trumpeter Swan: Success Story on the Wing

No one knows how many trumpeter swans used to inhabit North America — perhaps a hundred thousand, perhaps many times that number. But in 1932, there were believed to be only 69 in the entire country. Two-thirds of the survivors were in a single spot, the Centennial Valley and Red Rocks Lake in southern Montana; the rest were in Yellowstone Park a few miles to the east. There may also have been a tiny remnant somewhere in Canada, but for all practical purposes, the Greater Yellowstone ecosystem was the only spot left for this splendid bird, a creature weighing more than 20 pounds and with a wing span of eight feet. Greater Yellowstone was the trumpeter's final chance, the last place on earth where it could make it.

With the increased protection provided by the establishment of the Red Rocks National Wildlife Refuge in 1935, in conjunction with other conservation measures, the outlook for the swan improved. Within 15 years their numbers at Red Rocks and nearby areas climbed to 300. Today the magnificent trumpeter numbers about 10,000 and is frequently seen on the cold, clear streams, lakes and ponds of Yellowstone.

But even now, serious problems may lie ahead for the trumpeter in Greater Yellowstone, where its numbers are only stable at

the best estimate, or perhaps are declining. Its wintering areas on the Henry's Fork River are threatened with subdivision and second-home development, booming tourism and perhaps geothermal development. A more immediate concern is the possibility of reduced winter stream flows from Island Park Dam as a result of repair projects and perhaps hydro installation there. Should such reduced flows occur, the now open water of the Henry's Fork, which is home to the trumpeter, would freeze.

The fact that most of the surviving swans in 1932 were outside the boundaries of National Park itself is yet another example of why the larger area we call Greater Yellowstone is so important to wild land preservation in the area around the park, and why it is so important for the Greater Yellowstone ecosystem to survive intact.

Few sights in nature can match the grace and lovely lines of the trumpeter swan. (Barb and Mike Pflaum, top; Tom Murphy, bottom.)

The Bald Eagle: Fearsome Raptor with a Fragile Population

There are approximately 200 bald eagles in the Greater Yellowstone ecosystem, including about 50 breeding pairs. Prior to 1960, a precipitous decline in the eagle population occurred here, due largely to the indiscriminate use of DDT. By the early 1970s when DDT finally was banned, both the Yellowstone Park population unit and the unit inhabiting the upper Madison River, Red Rocks, and the Henry's Fork River had been decimated. Only along the Snake River in Jackson Hole, where DDT had not been sprayed, did the eagle population remain stable.

While the eagle population in Greater Yellowstone has recovered, the Yellow-

Without the protection of lands surrounding Yellowstone Park, such as Montana's Red Rocks National Wildlife Refuge (photo c), the bald eagles in the park proper face certain decline. (a, Paul Lally; b, Alan Carey; c, Wayne Scherr)

stone Park population remains fragile. Most of the park is still covered by snow and its lakes are frozen during the nesting months of March and April. In some years, the entire Yellowstone Park eagle unit may not produce a single new eagle. In a good year, perhaps half a dozen may be raised.

This means that the Yellowstone Park unit must depend heavily upon an influx of eagles from Jackson Hole and the Upper Henry's Fork-Red Rocks-Upper Madison unit. Unless eagle habitat in those areas is carefully protected, there can be no influx of eagles into Yellowstone Park, and without that, Yellowstone's eagles probably would decline in number dramatically and perhaps even disappear.

c

a

b

Greater Yellowstone Underground

As we consider the relationship between Yellowstone National Park and the surrounding lands, it becomes increasingly clear that we must take into account geological as well as ecological factors. The fabulous thermal areas of the park might be connected by subsurface systems to areas beyond the park boundary to the southwest and north. Commercial geothermal exploration and development have been proposed immediately adjacent to the southwest park boundary in an area known as the Island Park Geothermal Area.

Concern about such development so close to Yellowstone Park focuses on the question of what effect drilling there may have on the park's geysers, the rarest and most fragile of geothermal phenomena. In 1979 an elaborate environmental impact statement prepared by the U.S. Forest Service to consider the issue concluded: "The exact boundaries of the Yellowstone geothermal reservoir or reservoirs are uncertain, and no definite evidence is apparently available on what the permeability is at depth. Thus, it is hard to say how much of a connection, if any, there is between the possible geothermal resource of the Island Park Geothermal Area and thermal areas inside the park, or if any adverse effects might result."

Another area of interest to geothermal developers lies just north of the park boundary in the Corwin Springs Known Geothermal Resource Area. As in the case of Island Park, no one knows what connection may exist between the thermal systems of Yellowstone and the Corwin Springs geothermal area, but the answer may be important — Mammoth Hot Springs and its incomparable travertine terraces lies just four miles to the south.

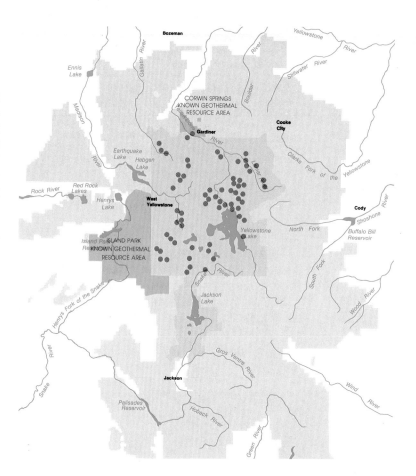

Geothermal Areas

Thermal Features

Hot Springs, Geysers

Known Geothermal Resource Areas (KGRA's)

National Parks

Other Federal Lands

Bubbling pots and steaming waters, pages in Yellowstone's explosive story. (Barbara and Michael Pflaum, top; Terrill Shorb, bottom)

These explosions and discharges, occur at intervals of about two hours. After having witnessed three of them, I ventured near enough to put my hand into the water of its basin, but withdrew it instantly, for the heat of the water in this immense couldron, was altogether to [sic] great for comfort, and the agitation of the water, disagreeable effluvium continually exuding, and the hollow unearthly rumbling under the rock on which I stood, so ill accorded with my notions of personal safety, that I retreated back precipately to a respectful distance. The Indians who were with me were quite appalled . . . One of them remarked that hell, of which he had heard from the whites, must be in the vicinity.

WARREN ANGUS FERRIS, 1834

North Grotto Fountain. (Fred Hirschmann)

The Political Fragmentation of Greater Yellowstone

In sharp contrast to the ecological (and possibly geological) relationships that tie the lands of Greater Yellowstone into one cohesive region, political and administrative boundaries untie the area and break it into a myriad of smaller unrelated jurisdictions (see map page 9). The millions of acres of national forest lands surrounding Yellowstone National Park lie on five different national forests, each with its own forest supervisor and separate administrative staff. Two of these forest supervisors (Targhee and Bridger-Teton) answer to a Forest Service regional office in Ogden, Utah; one answers to an office in Denver, Colorado (Shoshone); and two to an office in Missoula, Montana (Gallatin and Custer). Two wildlife refuges, the National Elk Refuge in Jackson, Wyoming near the southern end of Greater Yellowstone and Red Rocks National Wildlife Refuge near the western extent of Greater Yellowstone, are run by different managers who answer to a regional office in Denver.

Though most of Yellowstone National Park itself is in Wyoming, small portions are in Idaho and Montana. Three of the park entrances — West Yellowstone, Gardiner and Cooke City — are in Montana, while the east and south entrances are in Wyoming. The Greater Yellowstone Ecosystem spreads far into all three states and into portions of ten counties. Yellowstone and Grand Teton national parks have separate superintendents and administrative staffs. Yellowstone has exclusive federal jurisdiction (being created as a park long before Wyoming, Idaho or Montana became states), but park officials

Opposite page.
Top: The country of the Upper Yellowstone River. Yellowstone Lake is visible in the distance. (Rick Graetz)
Bottom: Wyoming Game and Fish Department patrol cabin in the Teton Wilderness. (U.S. Forest Service)

Above: The Teton Range from the west across Pierre's Hole near Driggs, Idaho. (Rick Reese)

Crossed the mountain 12 mls. East course and descended into the South W. extremity of a valley called Pierre's hole where we staid the next day. This valley lies north & South in an oblong form abt. 30 mls. long and 10 wide surrounded except on the Nth. by wild and rugged Mountains: the East range resembles Mountains piled on Mountains and capped with three spiral peaks which pierce the cloud. These peaks bear the French name of Tetons or Teats— The Snake Indians call them the hoary headed Fathers. This is a beautiful valley consisting of a Smooth plain intersected by small streams and thickly clothed with grass and herbage and abounds with Buffaloe Elk Deer antelope.

OSBORNE RUSSELL, 1835
in JOURNAL OF A TRAPPER

in Grand Teton must share jurisdiction with the Wyoming Game and Fish Department, Teton County, the Wyoming Highway Patrol, a local airport board and others. Add this geographical, political and administrative fragmentation to the dramatically differing mission charged to each of these agencies, and one begins to appreciate why the Greater Yellowstone area has never been managed as an ecological unit. That does not mean there is no cooperation among the various agencies; the Cooperative Elk Management Group and the Interagency Grizzly Bear Study Team are examples of good, joint-management undertakings. But in other instances cooperation between agencies has been lacking, leading to piecemeal administrative decisions with little consideration given to the Greater Yellowstone area as a whole.

Greater Yellowstone, then, is an enormous island of wild lands comprising America's largest essentially intact ecosystem existing outside Alaska; it is probably the largest such temperate-zone ecosystem remaining anywhere on earth. More than 95 percent of the area is public land entrusted to the stewardship of federal agencies but belonging to all Americans and of interest to the people of the world. Will that stewardship be exercised wisely and in a manner that will retain intact the biological communities of the ecosystem? Will it continue to supply the arid west with abundant pure water, protect forever the environmental integrity of Yellowstone National Park, and maintain a meaningful piece of America's wild-land heritage for the people of the third millenium and beyond? The American people must decide.

Pilot Peak in the North Absaroka Wilderness just south of Cooke City, Montana. (George Wuerthner)

Echo Peak in the new Lee Metcalf Wilderness near
the northwestern corner of Yellowstone Park. (Rick
Graetz)

Trying to manage wildlife in a wildlife community that is without its top predator is just no good.

DR. DURWOOD ALLEN
PURDUE UNIVERSITY WOLF SPECIALIST

Timber wolves on a deer carcass. (Alan Carey)

The Wolf: Missing Link

The wolf once reigned as the master predator of Yellowstone's large hoofed animals, but today it is gone from Yellowstone, the victim of a deliberate and highly successful extermination campaign, which began more than 100 years ago and continued for half a century with the official sanction of the guardians of the park — the U.S. Army and later the National Park Service. The extermination campaign, which extended to mountain lions, coyotes and wolverines, was based on the mistaken notion that some animals are good and some are bad, while the ungulates — elk, deer, moose, pronghorn, bighorn sheep and bison — were deemed good.

Appealing as such a notion may be to the uninformed, it can be a disaster to the ecological scheme of things. Wildlife biologists today know that predators are integral components of a biological balancing act, which, when given a chance, functions well in nature.

While inside Yellowstone itself man was protecting "good" ungulates from "bad" predators, outside the park livestock predation by wolves was the rationale for their extermination. It is ironic that the reason for man's war on the wolf stemmed almost entirely from one of man's other biological misdeeds, the decimation of the large herds of bison, which were the primary food source of the wolf at that time. The simultaneous introduction of domestic livestock into wolf range sealed the predator's fate as they were forced to turn from a diminishing native prey base to cattle and sheep. By 1925, the wolf essentially had been erased from the western landscape, and Yellowstone National Park was no exception. Since 1973, the wolf has been classified as an endangered species in the west.

The war against "bad" animals in the west utilized traps, guns and poisons. Between 1915 and 1941, the federal government's Bureau of Biological Survey killed 24,000 wolves in the western United States. Yellowstone was one of the last strongholds of the creature, but even here it was not safe. Between 1914 and 1926, at least 136 wolves were killed in the park. The natural process of thinning ungulate populations (especially elk) through predation by wolves upon the sick, old, weak, unwary, and occasionally upon healthy animals, had been short-circuited.

Many biologists believe that there are unnaturally high populations of elk in Yellowstone, though some Park Service researchers disagree. In a place where the forces of nature are left to operate without interference by man, every piece in the ecological puzzle is needed. To be sure the primary elk population regulator in Yellowstone National Park is winterkill, but the supplementary effect of wolf predation also may have been significant. Starvation of thousands of southern Yellowstone elk is prevented only by the intervention of feeding them hay at the National Elk Refuge at Jackson, Wyoming, and some researchers believe that native range in and near Yellowstone frequently is overgrazed by artificially large populations of elk. In areas outside Yellowstone, hunting mitigates some of the population pressures caused by lack of natural predation, but inside the park, where hunting is not allowed, the wolf is more sorely missed for whatever degree of elk predation it could provide.

One of the stated purposes of the National Park Service is to "conserve, perpetuate, and portray as a composite whole the indigenous ... terrestrial fauna." The intervention of man has taken the wolf from Yellowstone; perhaps it is time for man to return the wolf to a small fragment of its native habitat in Yellowstone National Park.

In 1980, the U.S. Fish and Wildlife Service approved a plan of the Northern Rocky Mountain Wolf Recovery Team to re-establish and maintain at least two viable populations of wolves in the northern Rocky Mountains. Given the needs of the wolf (most notably a year-round prey base, denning and rendezvous sites, and large areas of wild lands with minimal exposure to humans), the team was able to identify

Of all the native biological constituents of a northern wilderness scene, I should say that the wolves present the greatest test of human wisdom and good intentions.

PAUL L. ERRINGTON
in OF PREDATION AND LIFE

Given wise stewardship on the part of man, there appears to be enough room in the Yellowstone ecosystem for its creatures to work out their own peace.
(a) Pronghorn on the South Fork of the Shoshone River, Absaroka Mountains, Wyoming. (Barbara and Michael Pflaum)
(b) Mountain lion. (Alan Carey)
(c) Coyote. (Tim Christie)
(d) Golden eagle. (Alan Carey)
(e) River otter. (Tim Christie)
(f) Porcupine. (Ron Shade)

We have two million acres with elk running out our ears. It's a real set-up for wolves.

DR. DURWOOD ALLEN
PURDUE UNIVERSITY WOLF SPECIALIST

Winter-killed elk. (Tom Murphy)

only three geographic areas that could provide everything necessary for wolf recovery. One was Glacier National Park and the large system of wildlands stretching south along the Continental Divide into Montana; a second was in central Idaho and centered on the River of No Return, Selway-Bitterroot, and Gospel-Hump Wilderness areas; the third, and probably the most promising, was the Greater Yellowstone area.

While it appears that most wildlife biologists who have considered the matter strongly favor establishment of a wolf population in Greater Yellowstone, some vexing considerations have to be overcome before a viable wolf population once again will roam this country. One of these problems is socio-political rather than biological. To an American public brought up on the Three Little Pigs and Little Red Riding Hood, the wolf may not seem quite worthy of special favors (even though there is not a single documented case of an attack upon a human being by a healthy wolf in the entire history of the western United States). Livestock operators near Yellowstone might not be very enthusiastic about the return of the wolf either, yet strong support for the wolf is present in many quarters as the American public becomes better informed about the natural role of predation and of predators. Suffice it to say at this point, that in the absence of strong vocal public support for wolf recovery in Yellowstone, it won't happen.

Should the social and political climate be conducive for wolf recovery, the capture and transplanting of family units of wild wolves would be a difficult process. The Wolf Recovery Team has given much thought to how the wolves would be managed once transplanted. Their strategy is based on a zone system in which wolves

straying beyond certain areas would be captured or killed. In Zone I, probably limited to Yellowstone National Park and some nearby national forest lands, the wolf would be protected. Its habitat would be maintained and resource management decisions would favor the needs of the wolf. Zone II would serve as a buffer zone and travel corridor and would have some key habitat components, but not enough to sustain a viable wolf population. This area would include additional national forest lands around Yellowstone and the wolf would be considered as an important use, but not the primary use of the area. Wolf activity and its needs would be accommodated here, but not to the extent that they would preclude other high-priority land uses. Problem wolves would be controlled. Zone III would include areas beyond the corridor zone in which established human activities, such as livestock grazing, occur at a sufficient level to render wolf presence undesirable. The wolf would receive no extraordinary protection here, and conflicts with livestock and humans would be resolved against the wolf.

The biological case for returning the wolf to its former range in Greater Yellowstone is persuasive, but when the decision is made to go ahead with the re-establishment, it will be made only partly on biological grounds; political considerations will be at least as important.

Regardless of the merits of wolf re-establishment and its prospects for Greater Yellowstone, the fact that there is still a place left in the continental United States that meets the qualitative and quantitative wild land requirements of a wolf population, bespeaks again the extraordinary significance of this area. The wolf is gone, but its home remains essentially intact, ready for its return when the time comes.

Those sorts of political-scientific conundrums, allowed to continue, will eventually tear the Greater Yellowstone Ecosystem apart. There is so much we still don't know about it, and much we will never know. We all have our own ideas of how it's put together and where the rents must be mended, and some of us are right and some are wrong. But again, nobody is in charge. So I suggest we give it over to its best and highest use, and let it be a museum, a laboratory, a place to make a naturalist's eyes bug out of her head. And not just the park. Let them have the whole Greater Yellowstone Ecosystem.

GEOF O'GARA
in HIGH COUNTRY NEWS

Left: View from Ammerman Ridge in the Absaroka-Beartooth Wilderness south of Livingston. (Sandra McCune)
Below: Yellowstone River in Yellowstone Park. (Barbara and Mike Pflaum)

Part III

Threats to Greater Yellowstone

... the cultural and natural resources of the parks are endangered ... These threats, which emanate from both internal and external forces, are causing severe degradation of park resources.

STATE OF THE PARKS REPORT, NATIONAL PARK SERVICE

In May 1980, the Office of Science and Technology of the National Park Service completed the first comprehensive survey identifying threats to the natural and cultural resources of America's national parks. The report was prepared during the last months of the Carter Administration. Interior Secretary James Watt and other officials of the Reagan Administration were not enthusiastic about it.

The findings of the report are sobering and suggest a bleak future for many of our park lands. In terms of the total number of threats identified per park, Yellowstone ranks eighth among 310 national parks, monuments, and other units of the national park system. Perhaps more significantly, of the 12 parks in the United States that have been designated Biosphere Reserves by UNESCO in recognition of their global importance as representative ecosystems and irreplaceable genetic resources, Yellowstone is the second most threatened, exceeded only by Glacier National Park. As a group, these Biosphere Reserve parks, some of America's choicest ecosystems, average three times as many threats per park as non-biosphere reserve areas. Clearly, size, remoteness and fame are no guarantee against degradation.

"Without qualifications," the report says, "it can be stated that the cultural and natural resources of the parks are endangered both from without and from within by a broad range of such threats.... These threats which emanate from both internal and external forces are causing severe degradation of park resources."

More than half of the reported threats were attributed to sources or activities located outside the parks. These include logging, mining, oil and gas development, poaching, destruction of wildlife habitat, soil erosion, water and air pollution, roads and railroads, noise, encroachment of exotic plants and animals, off-road vehicle use and subdivisions. Other

Mr. Ingalls: The best thing that the Government could do with the Yellowstone National Park is to survey it and sell it as other public lands are sold.

Mr. Vest: The last hope of the preservation of the bison, the buffalo, the moose, and the elk upon the continent of North America exists in the preservation of that park, and to such an extent that it will be a great preserve... I am not ashamed to say that I shall vote to perpetuate this park to the American people. I am not ashamed to say that I think its existence answers a great purpose in our national life. There should be to a nation that will have a hundred million or a hundred and fifty million people a park like this as a great breathing-place for the national lungs...

DEBATE IN THE UNITED STATES SENATE, MARCH 1, 1883

September afternoon in the Hayden Valley, Yellowstone National Park. (Jeff Gnass)

threats identified in the report were associated with activities within the park boundaries, such as heavy visitor use, vehicle noise, and construction projects.

Clearly, all is not well with America's national parks as indicated in the bleak conclusion of the State of the Parks Report, which says: "There is no question that these threats will continue to degrade and destroy irreplaceable park resources until such time as mitigation measures are implemented. In many cases this degradation or loss of resources is irreversible. It represents a sacrifice by the public that, for the most part, is unaware that such a price is being paid."

Near the top of the list of those areas most threatened sits Yellowstone. The park and the Greater Yellowstone Ecosystem are inextricably linked. As the heart of that ecosystem, Yellowstone National Park cannot possibly survive unimpaired if the ecological unit of Greater Yellowstone is allowed to disintegrate. What is good for the Greater Yellowstone Ecosystem will be good for Yellowstone National Park.

The types of activities that threaten to disrupt the Greater Yellowstone Ecosystem vary widely. The threats inventory compiled for Yellowstone in the State of the Parks report identified 67 specific kinds of threats that were deemed harmful or probably harmful to Yellowstone—43 of the 67 were classified as threats originating partly or entirely outside Yellowstone's boundaries. Of these external threats, those posing the greatest potential for large-scale disruption included oil and gas exploration and development, logging, min-

ing, geothermal energy development, hydro power and reclamation projects, and resorts, subdivisions and recreational developments. Others, such as poor grazing practices, use of poisons and herbicides, power lines, over-use by humans, water pollution, and a series of political schemes to sell public lands and provide greater motor vehicle access to back country areas pose smaller threats that may nonetheless be highly significant.

The impact of these threats taken one at a time could be mitigated, but taken collectively, and in the absence of some immediate protective measures, their cumulative effect threatens to disrupt this system of wild lands to such degree that an irreversible degradation of the biological and geological communities of the Greater Yellowstone Ecosystem and Yellowstone National Park seems inescapable. A closer look at the nature of those activities and developments that are now occurring in Greater Yellowstone will help us understand why they forbode such large-scale degradation.

Oil and Gas Exploration and Development

Large areas of the Greater Yellowstone Ecosystem include geologic formations that many geologists believe are promising sites for the production of oil and gas. Parts of the western portion of the ecosystem lie within the so-called overthrust belt, a geologic formation of folded and faulted slabs of rock that have been thrust over younger rocks creating traps, which may contain oil and gas. Large discoveries of oil and gas have been made in the Canadian portion of the overthrust belt on the north and in the Wyoming portion on the south, causing intense interest to focus on the area in between including parts of Greater Yellowstone. Some of the eastern portion of the ecosystem is adjacent to areas of existing oil and gas activity. Geologists suspect that what they call the producing horizons of these areas lie under lands near the south and east boundaries of Yellowstone Park.

Mr. McAdoo: A land famine is approaching. Our population from natural causes and a tremendous wave of immigration is rapidly increasing...Here is a great wonderland to be preserved for the benefit of our people, for that innumerable caravan that every year go out to see in the great West the inspiring sights and mysteries of nature that elevate mankind and bring it into closer communion with omniscience; I believe this park should be preserved upon this, if for no other ground. The glory of this territory is its sublime solitude. Civilization is becoming so universal that man can only see nature in her majesty and primal glory, as it were, in these as yet virgin regions.

DEBATE IN THE UNITED STATES HOUSE OF REPRESENTATIVES, DECEMBER 14, 1886

Lower falls of the Yellowstone River. (Fred Hirschmann)

Oil and gas activity occurs in two major stages, exploration and subsequent development and production. During exploration a variety of geophysical investigations may be undertaken including mapping and gravitational, magnetic, and seismic prospecting. In remote back country locations, seismic prospecting frequently has meant detonating thousands of explosive charges along seismic lines, heavy helicopter traffic and increased human presence, all of which tend to disturb and sometimes displace wildlife populations. This is especially true in areas where criss-crossing and parallel seismic lines are shot across the same area over and over. This occurs in areas of high geophysical interest because findings are not shared among competing companies. Each must do its own investigation, even though the same area may have been tested repeatedly by others.

In areas where an operator has a lease and where preliminary exploration shows promise, exploratory drilling may be conducted. This usually means road construction, heavy truck traffic, leveling and clearing of drill sites, and possibly mud pits, camps, buildings and more people. If oil or gas is discovered, the area is then developed for production.

The activities associated with oil and gas development and production are of large magnitude. More and larger roads are constructed, and pipelines, utility lines, separators, generators, and storage tanks are built. Systems for pressure maintenance, waste disposal, recovery and communications are brought into the area along with more people and the elaborate support systems they require.

The environmental impact of such activities on wild lands can be devastating. A glimpse of how extensive these impacts may be is offered in a 1981 draft environmental impact

Top: The mountains of the Washakie Wilderness rise above a well in Wyoming's Four Bear Oil Field. (Bruce Hamilton)
Bottom: An oil drilling site on the Bridger-Teton National Forest. (U.S. Forest Service)

statement on the proposed leasing of the Washakie Wilderness Area, which abuts a portion of the Yellowstone Park boundary on the east. In a section entitled Summary of Adverse Impacts Which Cannot Be Avoided, the report predicted reduced wildlife winter range, declining populations of elk, moose, bighorn sheep (possibly below viable populations), large predators, and reduced wildlife habitat and displacement of many wildlife species. Other impacts mentioned included soil erosion, water pollution, loss of recreational opportunities, more traffic and increased motorized trespass on newly constructed roads. In a separate document dated September 14, 1981, Shoshone National Forest officials stated: "Oil and gas leasing [in Situation I bear areas] with its associated construction activities will have an adverse impact on the essential habitat and continued existence of the grizzly bear."

The late John Townsley, former superintendent of Yellowstone National Park, said of the proposal to lease the Washakie Wilderness: "The long term effects created by the impact of energy development would be devastating to the critical wildlife habitat and destroy the wilderness value in this wild, remote and incredibly scenic area adjoining Yellowstone National Park."

Once we understand the potential consequences of oil and gas development on the wild lands of Greater Yellowstone, we can begin to appreciate the magnitude of the problem. On the Bridger-Teton National Forest there are, at the time of this writing, approximately 1,600 oil and gas leases covering 2.3 million acres; 75 percent of the entire Targhee National Forest is leased or under lease application; half a million acres of the Washakie Wilderness is under lease application; 45,000 acres of the Gros Ventre area recommended for wilderness in RARE II has been leased; 20,000 acres of the Absaroka-

Since the exploration for oil intensified in 1981, we can't even find the elk to determine precise effects the energy activity is having on them.

DONALD ROY
WYOMING GAME & FISH DEPT. WILDLIFE BIOLOGIST

Beartooth Wilderness are under lease application; extensive areas of the Gallatin National Forest adjacent to Yellowstone National Park are under lease or lease application including 25,000 acres of essential grizzly bear habitat immediately adjacent to the Yellowstone Park boundary; there are numerous applications for areas wholly or partially within designated wilderness areas on the Shoshone National Forest; and during the past two years more than 4,000 miles of seismic exploration line have been shot on the Bridger-Teton National Forest by Amoco, Arco, Chevron, Shell, Mobil, Getty, Exxon, and nearly every other major oil company in the country. Thousands of leases and applications extending across millions of acres now cover much of the Greater Yellowstone Ecosystem. Former Secretary of the Interior James Watt ordered a speed-up in the processing of lease applications and between 1981 and 1982 the number of acres leased jumped from 97 million to 125 million with similar increases expected in 1983.

The impact of oil and gas drilling is not confined to the drilling sites. The increased pressure on wildlife by people—authorized and unauthorized—who use access roads is a primary concern. Top: Elk. Bottom: Moose. (photos by Peter and Alice Bengeyfield)

Greater Yellowstone Wilderness

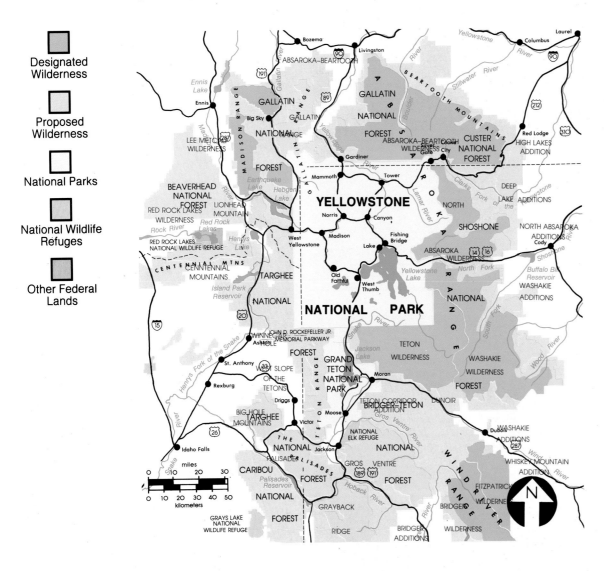

Legend:
- Designated Wilderness
- Proposed Wilderness
- National Parks
- National Wildlife Refuges
- Other Federal Lands

Current wilderness designation within the Greater Yellowstone ecosystem as a whole must continue. Only within designated wilderness does the grizzly bear have the security it needs to survive.

DR. JOHN CRAIGHEAD, 1982

Until recently it seemed that even congressionally-designated wilderness areas would be leased, explored and possibly drilled, but in 1982 Congress stepped in to prevent oil and gas development in wilderness and in areas recommended for wilderness during the RARE II process. Initially the measure provided only interim protection, but it recently was extended to stop leasing until the permanent ban, which was written into the Wilderness Act in 1964, became effective on January 1, 1984. The wilderness leasing issue came to the fore in 1980 when the Department of Interior asked the Shoshone National Forest to consider granting 72 lease applications pending at that time in the Washakie Wilderness. From the outset it was clear that the law allowed such leasing in wilderness even though it was unprecedented. Conservationists called it a legal loophole, but in a draft EIS the Forest Service recommended that 92,000 acres of the Washakie be open to oil and gas leasing and that 88 percent of the entire wilderness be open to geophysical exploration. The prospect of such leasing and the precedent it would set caused a storm of protest.

The congressional ban protects the four wilderness areas adjacent to Yellowstone National Park from oil and gas development as well as some areas officially recommended for wilderness designation, but it does nothing about millions of acres of non-wilderness, or about those leases already granted in wilderness or recommended wilderness. The proposed Gros Ventre Wilderness, southeast of Jackson Hole, Wyoming, is the largest single area in the lower 48 to be recommended as wilderness during the Rare II process. Wilderness designation for this extraordinary area was supported by 82 percent of those commenting during RARE II. Both the governor of Wyoming and the state Fish and Game Department support wilder-

Mr. Vest: The men who go there to a large extent are men of moderate means who cannot afford to go to Europe, but who desire in the rushing roar of active business life a vacation in the summer, and a place where they can rest their tired nerves and their overworked brains. I assert here again, there is not a trip in this country as cheap as to buy a round-trip ticket to the Yellowstone National Park, not one...

DEBATE IN THE UNITED STATES SENATE, MAY 10, 1892

Left: Fly fishing a remote backcountry stream in Yellowstone National Park. (Rick Reese)

Below: An early-morning climber looking north from the Grand Teton toward Mt. Moran and cloud-covered Jackson Hole, Wyoming. (Rick Reese)

The exact relationship between Yellowstone Park's thermal features and the hot water aquifer at the Island Park Geothermal Area to the west of the park is not known. However, geothermal energy developments in known thermal areas elsewhere in the world have a notorious record of destroying thermal features in areas in which drilling occurs. Here the Firehole River steams in winter.(Tom Dietrich)

ness here. But oil and gas leases already have been granted on 45,000 acres of the Gros Ventre and conservationists are locked in a battle to stop Getty Oil from drilling in the Little Granite Creek drainage of the Gros Ventre.

Outside of those areas covered by the congressional ban, nearly every acre of Greater Yellowstone that can be leased is leased, some of it in sensitive areas. Along the western boundary of Yellowstone, for example, near the town of West Yellowstone, leases recently were granted on 25,000 acres of the Gallatin National Forest, a considerable portion of which is in an area regarded by the Forest Service as essential grizzly habitat.

For the moment, no one knows if significant amounts of oil and gas will be found in the Greater Yellowstone Ecosystem, but if it is, everything is in place for development on a grand scale.

Geothermal Energy Development

Visitors to Yellowstone who take the time to attend an evening naturalist talk will learn that there is a great bubble of magma and hot rock underlying Yellowstone Park that provides the heat source to drive the park's unique thermal features. But what one might not be aware of is that other areas outside the park may also be underlain by hot rock, which is of great interest to geologists and to those who discern a potential for geothermal energy development.

There are three areas of particular interest

that geologists call Known Geothermal Resource Areas (KGRA): two, the Yellowstone KGRA and the Island Park KGRA, lie along the west and southwest boundary of Yellowstone; a third, the Corwin Springs KGRA, is adjacent to the north park boundary near Gardiner, Montana. (See map page 54) The relationship between the thermal features of Yellowstone and the nearby KGRA's outside the park are not well understood. It is suspected that these areas share a similar geologic history with Yellowstone, but unlike parts of Yellowstone where semi-molten magma lies relatively near the earth's surface, the KGRA's probably derive their thermal properties from residual heat in solid, but still hot, rock.

The Geothermal Steam Act of 1970 authorizes the leasing of national forest lands for geothermal exploration and development. In the Island Park Geothermal Area alone, more than 70 industrial and utility companies have applied for geothermal leases on some 77,000 acres of the Targhee National Forest. Leases already have been granted on 25,000 acres of state and private lands in the area. In response to this interest by energy developers, the U.S. Forest Service began an environmental impact study in 1975 to assess what geothermal development would mean for national forest land in the Yellowstone and Island Park KGRA's. In 1980 the Forest Service concluded that 37 percent of the Island Park Geothermal Area (IPGA) should be leased only if the Secretary of the Interior, in consultation with the Secretary of Agriculture, determined that there was a valuable geothermal resource there, that development of such a resource would not adversely affect the thermal features of Yellowstone National Park or the habitat of threatened or endangered wildlife species, and that air and water pollution would not affect other resource values of the area.

Great Fountain Geyser. (Charles Kay)

There is no geothermal development in the world within a geyser basin area that has been done without adverse effects on the geysers.

ROBERT HERBST
ASSISTANT SECRETARY OF THE INTERIOR, 1979

(a) Kayaker on an illegal trip down a portion of the Yellowstone River closed to boating. Park officials are currently wrestling with the safety, human impact and wildlife dilemmas that boating on the park's rivers would bring. (Mike Winfrey)
(b) White-water rafting on the Snake River below Jackson, Wyoming. (U.S. Forest Service)
(c) A wilderness guard's pack laden with garbage left by careless campers in the Absaroka-Beartooth Wilderness. (John Brandon)
(d) Snowmobilers and bison share the road in Yellowstone National Park. Visitors must take great care not to stress winter-weakened animals. (Charles Kay)
(e) A wary bighorn eyes a photographer. (Tim Christie)
(f) Forest Service patrol cabin in the Teton Wilderness. (U.S. Forest Service)

a

b

c

d

e

f

During the EIS process, concern focused immediately upon the danger that geothermal drilling at Island Park might affect the geysers and other thermal features of Yellowstone Park. The thermal features on upper Boundary Creek in Yellowstone National Park are only two miles from the IPGA; 13 other known thermal features are within 12 miles, and Old Faithful itself is only 13 miles distant. Concern is warranted—seven of the world's ten major geyser basins have been destroyed or seriously damaged by geothermal exploration or development. In New Zealand, the Geyser Thermal Valley, which ranked fifth among the major geyser areas on earth, died shortly after the Wairakei plant was installed nearby. In 1965 the last known geyser eruption occurred there, and in 1972 the Geyser Thermal Valley was closed as a tourist attraction. And the destruction of New Zealand's geyser fields has not been limited to the Geyser Thermal Valley. The December, 1982 newsletter of the New Zealand Geochemical Group reports that "There was a time when New Zealand had 130 geysers but now it has only five ..." The article goes on to document destruction of Papakura Geyser in 1975, and the final demise of Malfroy Geyser "immediately after drills were placed ..."

The destruction of geysers by geothermal drilling has not been limited to New Zealand. As the Island Park EIS notes, near cessation or total destruction of natural hot springs or geyser activity has occurred in Iceland, Italy and Nevada. The Beowawe Geysers of Nevada were second only to Yellowstone on the North American continent prior to geothermal exploration from 1945 to 1958. During that period wells were drilled, and by 1961 all springs and geysers had ceased flowing. The geysers of Steamboat Springs, Nevada were similarly destroyed by the early 1960s.

It is important to note that although thermal areas are not particularly unusual, geysers are extremely rare and are the most fragile of all geothermal phenomena. They require the occurrence of a highly unusual combination of factors and are easily disrupted. The case for extreme caution in Yellowstone is strong. It is the greatest concentration of geysers in the world (there are more geysers here than on the rest of the earth combined) and it is probably the only major undisturbed geyser area left on earth.

It is simply not known if there is a connection between the thermal features of Yellowstone Park and the IPGA. America's best geologists are unwilling to guarantee that drilling in the IPGA will not affect the thermal features of Yellowstone. According to geologist Duncan Foley, a specialist in geothermal geology, "Anybody who says they have an absolute answer is overstating his case. Nobody agrees because nobody knows for sure."

The most recent research, however, now indicates a greater likelihood of a connection than previously thought. Studies by the University of California in the southwest corner of Yellowstone during the summer of 1983 show the possibility of a much deeper heat source than most scientists had suspected. These findings suggest the presence of a local hot-water reservoir originating in the southwestern portion of Yellowstone. Research by the United States Geothermal Survey in the same area shows a conducting layer at shallow depth, which is consistent with a hot-water aquifer that may extend into the IPGA. Both findings point to a likely connection between the thermal features inside Yellowstone and the Island Park area.

Largely as a result of the controversy surrounding Island Park, Congress has taken an interest in the matter. In February 1983, the late Senator Henry Jackson introduced a bill that would amend the Geothermal Steam Act of 1970 to ban geothermal leasing until the Secretary of the Interior determined that exploration and development would not have "a foreseeably significant adverse affect on nationally significant geothermal features." Another provision of the bill singles out the IPGA for a two-year study to determine if drilling there would harm the thermal features of Yellowstone Park. To make such a determination in two years is ambitious indeed given the fact that some of the best minds in the field of geology have been unable to determine if a geothermal resource even exists in the IPGA.

Aside from its potential impact on Yellowstone's thermal features, geothermal development raises other concerns for Yellowstone Park and the Greater Yellowstone Ecosystem. During the geothermal exploration stage, test wells are drilled. This means the use of truck-mounted drill rigs and compressors or water trucks. They need roads, they need drill pads, they need generators and sump pits and mud tanks and people.

Nearly 20 percent of the IPGA is in Situation I grizzly bear habitat and Dick Knight, leader of the Interagency Grizzly Bear Study Team, was quoted more than ten years ago as saying, "This geothermal development is the worst thing that can happen to the grizzly bear."

This mule deer died tangled in a barbed wire fence just outside Yellowstone National Park. (Charles Kay)

Fifty percent of the resident trumpeter swans winter within the IPGA; the endangered bald eagle and possibly the peregrine falcon find their homes here as do prairie falcons, ferruginous hawks, sharptail grouse, and possibly remnant populations of Canada lynx, fishers and wolverines. The open waters of the Henry's Fork River are, in the words of the U.S. Fish and Wildlife Service, "the primary wintering area of all of Canada's trumpeter swans." From a fisheries standpoint, the Henry's Fork itself is probably the most important stream in Idaho.

But perhaps most portentious of all is the prospect of well-mouth power plants and their enormous associated impacts that would come to the boundary of Yellowstone if an exploitable geothermal resource were found here. That could mean full-scale industrialization for the future of Island Park.

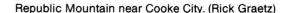
Republic Mountain near Cooke City. (Rick Graetz)

Most of these great parks were at one time pristine areas surrounded and protected by vast wilderness regions. Today, with their surrounding buffer zones gradually disappearing, many of these parks are experiencing significant and widespread adverse effects associated with external encroachment.

STATE OF THE PARKS REPORT, 1980

Logging

For years logging on the forests of the Greater Yellowstone Ecosystem was done on a relatively small scale by local operators. But with the arrival of large national and international wood products corporations in the area in the mid-'50s, cutting doubled, then doubled again by the mid-'60s. During this period enormous clear-cuts were made on the forests of the west.

About half of the national forest immediately adjacent to Yellowstone's boundary is in designated wilderness and therefore not available for timber sales. But the other half is not protected from logging and it is here that past, current and projected future logging practices are of concern. The United States Forest Service is in the business of selling timber: the law provides that the government should be managing its forests on a sustained-yield basis; that is, it shouldn't allow cutting of more than is being replaced with new growth. But the pressure to cut more timber, even where the government loses money on the sale, has grown steadily and today it has reached a new high. The Reagan administration has proposed a national timber cut of 11 billion board feet for 1984, up sharply from 6.2 billion board feet in 1982 and a predicted 8.5 billion board feet in 1983. At a time when the budget for timber sales and road building is going up 14 percent, only one-third of scheduled expenditures for wildlife and fish habitat improvement have been funded; funds for reforestation and planting of new trees will drop 40 percent.

To be sure, the emphasis on logging to the exclusion of wildlife, recreation and other values is nothing new in the Forest Service, an agency that employs nearly 6,000 foresters and only 523 wildlife biologists, and the increased intensity of timber cutting on our national forest will not abate in the near future if the statements of John Crowell, Assistant Secretary of Agriculture in charge of the Forest Service, are any indication. Crowell says he wants the Forest Service to double the timber cut on our national forests between now and the end of the century.

In the Greater Yellowstone Ecosystem logging is of concern in several areas. Foremost among these is the Targhee National Forest which completely surrounds the southwest corner of Yellowstone National Park. (See satellite photo on page 37.). The largest timber sale ever made outside Alaska was made here on the Moose Creek Plateau adjacent to Yellowstone. The sale totalled 318 million board feet of timber, and when the last tree falls more than a hundred square miles of the area will have been cut. Forest Service officials explain that much of the lodgepole pine on the Targhee near Yellowstone has been attacked by the pine beetle and is dead or dying and therefore needs to be cut now to salvage it from loss. In the four years between 1974 and 1978, the cut on the Targhee tripled.

The policy of accelerated cutting on the Targhee on the basis of beetle infestation may mean that other resource values, notably wildlife, are being sacrificed. A recently released Targhee National Forest Plan states that for the areas adjacent to Yellowstone on the west: "A heavy short-term impact on wildlife habitat and visual resources will occur in order to accelerate salvage and regeneration of lodgepole pine stands killed by the mountain pine beetle." The plan notes that logging will affect 7,200 acres of Situation I grizzly bear habitat each year.

Forest creeps to the edge of
the Gibbon River in the park.
(Jeff Gnass)

I don't consider Yellowstone Park as an island that can be self-perpetuated...All these activities in combination become a tremendous threat to Yellowstone.

JOHN TOWNSLEY
SUPERINTENDENT OF YELLOWSTONE NATIONAL PARK, 1975—1982

Right: Logging operation on the Teton National Forest. (U.S. Forest Service)
Far right: Slash burning on the Targhee National Forest. (Rick Reese)

Another section of the plan says that "large sales will be offered first in areas where the most live lodgepole is likely to be killed by the pine beetle." So it seems the Forest Service has developed a rationale for cutting all the trees: Cut the beetle-killed trees for salvage and cut the live lodgepole that might be beetle killed. In a lodgepole forest, that's all the trees.

Elsewhere in the plan, Forest Service officials note that certain wildlife species depend on old-growth trees for habitat, and it is therefore proposed that a mere 97 percent rather than 100 percent of all timberlands here be cut.

In the Gallatin National Forest, northwest of Yellowstone, highly controversial timber-cutting programs are being conducted by both the Forest Service and the Burlington Northern company. Burlington Northern owns tens of thousands of acres intermingled with national forest land in a checkerboard pattern, and the company is cutting in several areas to supply logs for its subsidiary, Plum Creek Lumber Company, and other mills.

In upper Sunlight Creek on the Shoshone National Forest within a few miles of the Yellowstone Park boundary and the North Absaroka Wilderness Area, hundreds of acres were cut in 1983 in the midst of grizzly country.

What does all this logging in the Greater Yellowstone area mean for Yellowstone National Park and the Greater Yellowstone Ecosystem? Several major impacts accompany logging operations in the slow-growth forests of the intermountain west. The most obvious and perhaps the most deleterious over the long run is the construction of roads into areas previously inaccessible by motor vehicles. Roads usually bring dramatically increased human presence that for many wildlife species can be disastrous. Cover, birthing areas, and other forms of sanctuary are lost. Migration routes often are disrupted, greater pressure occurs on wildlife to avoid humans, and hunting pressure increases. The net effect is frequently a decline in wildlife population. Displacement of the animals to other areas may occur if such areas are available, but as the cumulative pace of development in Greater Yellowstone accelerates, those neighboring areas already may be occupied by oil rigs, ski lifts, summer homes, motorcycles or mines. Roads can have other less obvious, but nonetheless serious, consequences. Soil and vegetation are disturbed, resulting in erosion and stream sedimentation, which is further compounded by skidding and timber removal once the logging operation itself begins.

Once the roads are in and the logs are out, the altered vegetative cover of the land becomes yet another concern. In many instances, the new vegetation in logged areas provides more abundant feed for wildlife than was available in the forested areas. This can be locally beneficial, but across an entire forest or region more sanctuary frequently is lost and more human pressure is gained to offset the benefit of short-term browse.

On the Targhee National Forest, yet another concern related to logging and the heavy potential impacts that can extend far beyond logged areas, is the use of poison grain to kill gophers, which eat the seedlings in reforestation efforts. The effect of such poison on bears, birds of prey and other species that eat the poisoned gophers may be a serious matter. Likewise, the use of pesticides to control insects and diseases where other methods cannot be used or are not cost effective is called for in the Targhee Forest Plan as is the use of herbicides to destroy plants that compete with tree reproduction in logged areas.

We need logs from our national forests. Whether we need the volume of logs we are taking from the Targhee at this time and in this place, next door to Yellowstone, and whether roads, sedimentation and poison are the best way to treat this land is a question that should be of interest to all concerned about the future of Greater Yellowstone.

Above left: Colter Peak on the southeastern boundary of Yellowstone Park. (Wayne Scherr)
Above right: Stormy afternoon in the Absaroka-Beartooth Wilderness. (John Brandon)

The National Parks do not suffice as a means of perpetuating the larger carnivores; witness the precarious status of the grizzly bear, and the fact that the park system is already wolfless. Neither do they suffice for mountain sheep; most sheep herds are shrinking.

The reasons for this are clear in some cases and obscure in others. The parks are certainly too small for such a far-ranging species as the wolf. Many animal species, for reasons unknown, do not seem to thrive as detached islands of population.

The most feasible way to enlarge the area available for wilderness fauna is for the wilder parts of the National Forests, which usually surround the Parks, to function as parks in respect of threatened species. That they have not so functioned is tragically illustrated in the case of the grizzly bear.

ALDO LEOPOLD
A SAND COUNTY ALMANAC, 1948

Mr. Toole: Mr. Chairman...I undertake to say that the passage of this bill [to grant a railroad right of way through Yellowstone National Park] is absolutely a commercial necessity...It is wholly an unattractive country. There is nothing whatever in it, no object of interest to the tourist, and there is not one out of twenty who ever visits for purposes of observation this remote section.

Mr. Cox: Mr. Chairman, I believe this bill is wrongly entitled. It should be denominated "A bill for the spoilation of this Yellowstone Park."
This is a measure which is inspired by corporate greed and natural selfishness against national pride and natural beauty! It is a shame to despoil this park for mere mercenary purposes, such as running a railroad to these mines...

DEBATE IN THE UNITED STATES HOUSE OF REPRESENTATIVES, DECEMBER 14, 1886

Top: Decayed mining shack at Goose Lake in the Absaroka-Beartooth Wilderness. (Sherry Funke)
Bottom: Hikers explore an abandoned mining camp including a '49 woody above Cooke City. (Sherry Funke)

Mining

In 1872 Congress passed a mining law that opened public domain lands to mineral prospecting and granted miners the right to claim minerals and the surface over such minerals for private purposes. In 1897 the law was broadened to include national forest lands.

So-called potential mining claims give the claimant full ownership and control of both minerals and the surface. This, in essence, converts public land to private property. For many decades claims were patented easily and the requirement that a claimant demonstrate a valuable mineral body on the claim was not monitored carefully or enforced by the government. Many of the private inholdings in today's wilderness areas, national parks and wildlife refuges were conveyed from the government to private parties as patented mining claims. Unpatented mining claims, on the other hand, grant only ownership of minerals, but not of the surface; surface ownership is retained by the government, and federal agencies have some say about how the surface resources are managed.

The 1872 mining law was passed at a time when mineral development and exploration was conducted primarily by individuals and small operators. It provided for the give-away of public minerals and public lands on a first-come basis. There was no competitive bidding for claimable minerals, and there still isn't even today. Anyone can file an unpatented mining claim on national forest land. This right extends even to wilderness areas, which were open to claim until January 1, 1984. After that date no new claims would be granted in wilderness, but existing valid claims may be worked.

In recent years, the 1872 mining law has come under attack by conservation organizations that contend that it grants far too much latitude to miners at the expense of the public interest, especially on the national forests of the west. Under the law, anyone may stake a claim on national forest land; occupy and use the land for prospecting, mining and processing ore; clear timber on the claim and cut it for use in mining; barter, sell or mortgage their claim just as any other real property may be bought and sold. Perhaps most importantly the law grants access across other public lands when it is necessary to reach a claim on the national forest. For this the claimant pays the government nothing.

The law does require that a miner do a minimum of $100 per year worth of "assessment work" to maintain a valid claim, and also requires a miner to show that there is some valuable mineral or a good prospect of finding a valuable mineral on the claim. In practice, this last requirement is rarely enforced because the Forest Service has only a few mineral specialists to inspect thousands of claims. The Forest Service does, however, have the authority to require miners to conduct their operation in a manner that will minimize damage to the national forest, but such conditions may not "materially interfere" with the prospector's operations.

Mining claims, patented and unpatented, cover a large area of Greater Yellowstone. The greatest concentration of claims is clustered around the northeast corner of the park, throughout the Shoshone National Forest east of the park, and on the southeast, inside and adjacent to the Washakie Wilderness Area (See map page 82.) The Forest Service estimates there are more than 2,300 mining claims in the North Absaroka and Washakie wildernesses and 380 claims in the Absaroka-Beartooth Wilderness. Most of these claims are not being worked at present,

but higher metal prices could quickly fuel a mining boom in the area.

In the area southeast of Yellowstone, right on the boundary of the Washakie Wilderness at Kirwin, American Metals Climax Inc. has been planning a particularly large-scale mining operation for more than 10 years. Depressed copper prices are keeping the project on the back burner for now, but when it comes, it will be a massive open-pit mine with a large mill site, waste dump, new roads and perhaps a 20-mile slurry pipeline across a roadless portion of the Shoshone National Forest. The proposed project is on the upper Wood River in prime wildlife habitat with an estimated population of 1,000 deer, 150 elk and numerous bighorn sheep and moose. A company-funded study on the project con-

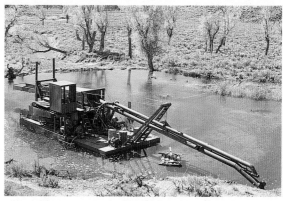

Top: A portion of the Absaroka Range near Deer Creek Pass. (Barbara and Michael Pflaum)
Bottom: Gold dredge on Cottonwood Creek in the Gros Ventre Mountains. (U.S. Forest Service)

Areas of Mining Interest

☐ National Parks

☐ Other Federal Lands

☐ Designated Wilderness

☐ Proposed Wilderness

▨ Areas of Mining Interest

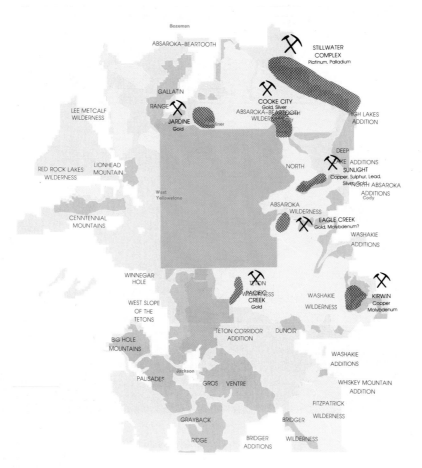

Bozeman

ABSAROKA-BEARTOOTH

STILLWATER COMPLEX
Platinum, Palladium

GALLATIN RANGE

COOKE CITY
Gold, Silver
ABSAROKA-BEARTOOTH WILDERNESS

HIGH LAKES ADDITION

JARDINE
Gold

LEE METCALF WILDERNESS

RED ROCK LAKES WILDERNESS

LIONHEAD MOUNTAIN

DEEP LAKE ADDITIONS
SUNLIGHT
Copper, Sulphur, Lead, Silver, Gold
NORTH ABSAROKA ADDITIONS
Cody

NORTH

West Yellowstone

CENNTENNIAL MOUNTAINS

ABSAROKA WILDERNESS

EAGLE CREEK
Gold, Molybdenum?

WASHAKIE ADDITIONS

WINNEGAR HOLE

TETON WILDERNESS
PACIFIC CREEK
Gold

WASHAKIE WILDERNESS

KIRWIN
Copper Molybdenum

WEST SLOPE OF THE TETONS

TETON CORRIDOR ADDITION

DUNOIR

BIG HOLE MOUNTAINS

WASHAKIE ADDITIONS

Jackson

PALISADES

GROS VENTRE

WHISKEY MOUNTAIN ADDITION

FITZPATRICK WILDERNESS

GRAYBACK RIDGE

BRIDGER

BRIDGER ADDITIONS

WILDERNESS

claims in the Sunlight Basin, an important elk calving and recreation area, which is also prime grizzly habitat. Higher up Sunlight Creek, just a few miles from Yellowstone's eastern boundary, active mining is occurring in the Silvertip Basin area of the North Absaroka Wilderness Area.

During the latter quarter of the 19th century and first two decades of the 20th century, Cooke City, Montana underwent a mining boom that produced substantial quantities of silver and gold. But mining activity there also poisoned Soda Butte Creek with acid mine drainage for miles into Yellowstone National Park. Today, a Washington company is talking about reworking mine tailings throughout this area.

North across the park boundary, about 35 miles due west of Cooke City near Jardine, Montana, Homestake Mining plans to begin work on a large gold mine early in 1985. It is projected to produce 750 tons of ore a day. The entire mine site is on a watershed that drops directly into the Yellowstone River, a significant factor given the enormous arsenic wastes that accumulated here as a result of past mining activities. To their credit, Homestake and the Anaconda Company (the previous owner of the Jardine property) have removed a thousand tons of the arsenic wastes to a hazardous-waste site in Idaho. Homestake's operation at Jardine will employ 150 miners and swell the population of tiny Gardiner, Montana by perhaps twice that number.

Mining has a less concentrated impact on many other areas of Greater Yellowstone. From the claims in the Absaroka-Beartooth Wilderness on the north, to the gold lode near Pacific Creek in the Teton Wilderness on the south, the impact or potential impacts are the same: roads, drills, motor vehicles, heavy equipment, excavation, erosion and people, always more people.

tended that scenery in the area might actually be enhanced by the mining, which would remove the top of 12,012-foot Bald Mountain, "therefore affording a better view of the more impressive Spar Mountain" about a mile to the east.

To the west of Kirwin, closer to Yellowstone and inside the Washakie Wilderness, other claims, mostly unpatented, are being explored. Exploratory drilling has been completed or proposed on claims near Needle Creek, Silver Creek, in the Dead Horse area and on the Dunrud Claims. To the north, Exxon recently has explored with truck-mounted drill rigs on 245 unpatented mining

Opposite page: Ferrous hydroxide from an old mining operation near Cooke City, Montana pollutes a tributary of Soda Butte Creek a few miles before it flows into Yellowstone Park. (N. A. Bishop) Above: Alpine lake in the Beartooth Mountains, Shoshone National Forest, Wyoming. (Jeff Gnass)

Gibbon Falls in Yellowstone Park. (Peter and Alice Bengeyfield)

Water and Hydro Projects

The Greater Yellowstone area is one of North America's largest watersheds. In its mountains are found the headwaters of the Missouri River (including the Yellowstone, Madison, Gallatin, Clark's Fork of the Yellowstone, Shoshone and Grey Bull rivers), the Columbia River (including the Snake and Henry's Fork rivers), and the Green River.

For nearly a hundred years promoters and developers have had their eyes on Yellowstone's waters. As early as 1893 a serious scheme was put forth to utilize the waterfalls of Yellowstone National Park to generate electricity. In 1920 a plan to dam the Bechler Meadow in the southwest corner of the park was vigorously pursued, and that same year a dam was proposed for the Yellowstone River in Yankee Jim Canyon a few miles north of the park boundary. Every year between 1920 and 1924, Congress considered proposals to dam the Yellowstone River three miles below its outlet from Yellowstone Lake at Fishing Bridge; in 1926 a bill was introduced in Congress to omit the Bechler country in the southwest corner of the park from Yellowstone so the Bechler River could be dammed; and in the early '30s a plan was put forth to divert water from Yellowstone Lake to Shoshone Lake, then through tunnels into Idaho. In every instance congressional and public sentiment for the preservation of Yellowstone's rivers and lakes won out, but in some cases the forces for water projects were strong and the outcome was not secured easily.

Beyond the park boundary but well within the Greater Yellowstone Ecosystem, dams were built: on the Snake River at Jackson Hole, on the Henry's Fork at Island Park, on the Madison at Hebgen and Ennis lakes, and on a smaller scale at numerous locations. But today thousands of miles of waterways in the Greater Yellowstone Ecosystem continue as free-flowing, relatively natural rivers, streams and lakes. The Yellowstone River itself remains undammed throughout its entire course from its headwaters above Yellowstone Lake in the Teton Wilderness to its confluence with the Missouri River near the Montana-North Dakota border. Many proposals have been put forth to dam the Yellowstone. By far the largest and most serious of these proposals is the one that would dam the Yellowstone River at Allen Spur 50 miles north of Yellowstone Park, just two miles above Livingston, Montana. Pursued at various times by federal agencies during the past several decades, the water impounded by a dam at Allen Spur would flood nearly the entire length of Montana's Paradise Valley.

The Bureau of Reclamation has a more imminent plan, which could involve building a new dam on the Snake River three miles below the Jackson Lake Dam. This proposal was put forth as a result of investigations showing that the existing dam may be vulnerable to liquefaction when subjected to seismic tremors. This means the dam would fail as its saturated soils lost strength and flowed as a fluid. The proposed new dam would cost at least $38 million and flood an additional 2,000 acres of Grand Teton National Park, including the priceless riparian areas at the Oxbow of the Snake River. Another and perhaps a more likely option suggested by the bureau would be to repair the existing dam at an estimated minimum cost of $82 million. The project's technical feasibility is questionable and would entail a monumental four-year construction

project in the heart of the Grand Teton National Park. Those opposing the new dam and the repair option have suggested water conservation measures and a drought-insurance program that would allow lowering the level of Jackson Lake 19 feet at which point failure of the dam would not pose a serious risk.

There are a variety of hydropower and reclamation projects proposed for the waters of the Greater Yellowstone Ecosystem. A look at one area, the Henry's Fork River and its tribu-

The seeming tranquility of Yellowstone Lake conceals the fact that rising geologic formations near its north end are tilting the lake so rapidly that trees along its south shore are drowning. Though the uplift of 10 to 12 mm. per year that has occurred over the last 50 years may seem slight, on the scale of geologic time it represents an almost instantaneous change. (Fred Hirschmann)

The Clark's Fork Canyon on the Shoshone National Forest north of Cody, Wyoming was carved by t
Fork of the Yellowstone River, which drops through here at a rate of more than 100 feet per mile. In
forest service proposed that 21 miles of the river be designated a national wild and scenic river. The
is pending in Congress. (George Wuerthner)

a

(a) Trumpeter swan pair. (Barb and Mike Pflaum)
(b) Fairy Falls, Yellowstone National Park. (Tom Dietrich)
(c) Mesa Falls on the Henry's Fork River of Idaho, where a hydro-electric dam has been proposed. (Sherry Funke)

b

c

> ... that disgusting dam...it has destroyed the august serenity of the lake's outlet forever; and has defaced and degraded the shores of the lake where once the pines grew green and dark.
>
> OWEN WISTER, DESCRIBING JACKSON LAKE DAM, 1936

(a) A hydro diversion on the Teton River in Idaho which resulted in total dewatering of the stream. (Idaho Department of Fish and Game)
(b) Jackson Lake Dam. (National Park Service)
(c) The Reas Pass powerline running between Mack's Inn, Idaho and West Yellowstone, Montana, an area described by the Interagency Grizzly Bear Study Team as habitat highly desired by bears. (Rick Reese)

taries, which lie just west of the Yellowstone Park boundary, illustrates the implications of such projects for the fish, wildlife, recreation and water quality of this part of the country.

In 1978 Congress passed the National Energy Act. One section of the act directed the Federal Energy Regulatory Commission (FERC) to formulate rules that would encourage small power production. In 1980 the agency required utility companies to purchase power generated by small producers at a favorable price. By providing a guaranteed market at a favorable price, much of the risk of hydro development was removed. As a result, permit applications to tie up development sites for hydro projects increased from 38 in 1979 to nearly 2,000 in 1981.

The Henry's Fork River is probably the finest stretch of fly fishing water in all of Idaho and is universally recognized as one of the world's premier trout fisheries. It is also home to 80 percent of the fragile tri-state trumpeter swan flock which depends heavily upon steady winter stream flows for ice-free winter habitat. On the Henry's Fork and its major tributaries today there are at least 15 proposed hydro-power projects, all of which pose potential for significant fisheries damage through dewatering of streams, destruction of spawning areas, interruption of fish passage, and loss of fish to turbines. Additional aesthetic impacts, especially at some particularly scenic sites such as Upper and Lower Mesa Falls, also can be expected. Major projects proposed for the area include the instal-

lation of hydro facilities at the Island Park Dam, at Sheep Falls on the Henry's Fork River where application has been made for a permit and water rights, at three additional sites upstream of Sheep Falls, at both Upper and Lower Mesa Falls on the Henry's Fork, on the Warm River where the stream would be dewatered and diverted through a penstock and on the Falls River.

No one knows what will come of the hydro proposals for the Henry's Fork and its tributaries, but as in so many other instances in Greater Yellowstone today, the potential for development is there, and the rate at which it occurs will in all likelihood be based on economic rather than environmental considerations.

Other Threats

While oil and gas development, geothermal energy, logging, mining, and water projects pose some of the largest threats to the Greater Yellowstone Ecosystem, a myriad of other activities and developments are underway that are less noticeable and of smaller scale, but are relentlessly chipping away at the environmental integrity of Greater Yellowstone.

Recreational resorts and subdivisions, many of which are located in prime lowland, riparian and wildlife winter-range areas, dot the landscape. Major ski areas at Teton Village near Jackson, Wyoming, Grand Targhee on the west slope of the Tetons, and Big Sky south of Bozeman, have had significant impacts in terms of the number of people they attract to the area as well as the physical impact of facility construction. Other resorts are being planned. Sleeping Giant, just two miles from the east entrance of Yellowstone Park, plans a major expansion to serve five times as many skiers per day as currently use the facility. The entire area is located on public land in prime grizzly bear habitat. The Shoshone National Forest has given the go-ahead to the expansion, citing economic benefits and down playing potential negative impacts on water quality, soil stability and wildlife disturbance. At Hebgen Lake north and west of West Yellowstone, an application for construction of the massive Ski Yellowstone project has been approved after ten years of controversy. When complete, this four-season resort and recreation subdivision will include ten ski lifts, a gondola, a mountain-

Bison silhouetted by early morning light reflected on Yellowstone Lake near Bridge Bay. (Fred Hirschmann)

The national park system, one of the major talismans of the United States as a civilized community, is in trouble. Desperate trouble.

The Late REP. PHILLIP BURTON

(a) The black bear, in spite of its stereotyped image, is rarely seen these days begging near the roadside in Yellowstone Park. The bear, now denied garbage, must find his niche in the natural system along with the rest of the park's animals.
(b) Mule deer, having dropped their antlers by mid-December, may look thin and weak through the winter. By autumn they are pictures of speed and agility.
(c) Although often incorrectly called antelope, pronghorn reside in a scientific category all their own, antilocapridae.
(Tim Christie photos)

top restaurant and ski runs on 1,800 acres of Mount Hebgen, all of which lie on federal lands of the Gallatin National Forest in occupied grizzly bear habitat. On 1,100 acres of adjacent private land, two enormous villages will be constructed, one at the base of Mount Hebgen, the other across the road from Hebgen Lake. Together, the two planned village facilities include 600 hotel rooms, nearly 500 condominiums, 224 private homes and 225 units of employee housing for a total overnight capacity of 4,920 persons! Development on this scale portends great changes for the Mount Hebgen area, which will be converted from a sparsely populated, mostly natural area, to a densely populated urban-style recreational development. In recommending the project, Gallatin National Forest officials noted that "there will be a great influx of money into the county," and that "many more people will benefit from construction of this ski area than would benefit from non-development. Few people," the report concluded "will be adversely impacted by the development."

At hundreds of other locations throughout Greater Yellowstone, large acreages are being subdivided and converted from open space to recreational second homes and condominiums as man spreads out and further encroaches onto the natural face of the ecosystem. The rate of population growth in some areas of Greater Yellowstone is simply staggering. In 1950, mostly agricultural Teton County, Wyoming, for example, had less than 2,600 residents. Today at least 12,000 people inhabit the county and agriculture has declined steadily constituting only a small percentage of the local economy. Most significantly the population there is growing at 12 percent a year, a rate at which the population will double every six years.

South of the proposed Ski Yellowstone development a new 115-kilovolt power line between Mack's Inn, Idaho and West Yellowstone has just been completed. Part of the stated justification cited for the line was possible new demand for electricity at Ski Yellowstone and at new subdivisions in West Yellowstone. The selected route across Reas Pass traverses a portion of Situation I grizzly bear habitat, an area described by the Interagency Grizzly Bear Study Team as "habitat highly desired by bears." An alternative route along an existing power line and utility corridor was rejected in part because it would cost more, even though the U.S. Fish and Wildlife Service strongly recommended it.

Meanwhile in the northern end of the Greater Yellowstone Ecosystem, another power line threatens, this one between Big Sky and Ennis, Montana through Jack Creek in the Madison Range. This area, bitterly contested between conservationists and those who favor construction of the road and power line, cuts the newly created Lee Metcalf Wilderness in two. It now appears that Jack Creek will get its road and power line as part of a trade-off for creation of the Lee Metcalf Wilderness.

Livestock grazing allotments on National Forest land throughout the Greater Yellow-

(a) Aerial tramway towers at Teton Village, Wyoming. (U.S. Forest Service)
(b) Subdivision encroaching on agricultural land south of Jackson, Wyoming. (Charles Kay)
(c) Mule deer in the Gardiner River mutilated for antlers. (Charles Kay)
(d) Vandalism of thermal features in the Midway Geyser Basin. (Charles Kay)

(a) Sheep grazing on the Targhee National Forest, Idaho. (U.S. Forest Service)
(b) A high lake in the Absaroka-Beartooth Wilderness, Montana. (Rick Graetz)
(c) Cross-country ski campers in the Bechler River country of southwestern Yellowstone National Park. (Rick Reese)

stone area have been issued for decades. Many of these are held by responsible ranchers who graze the public land in accordance with sound range-management principles. In other instances, however, private operators have ravaged public range lands. On one area in the North Absaroka Wilderness Area a forest service report notes "heavy and severe" grazing impacts where "over-utilization by livestock occurs and results in inadequate forage remaining for elk and transitional range, and in prime components of grizzly bear habitat." The Targhee

National Forest has categorized 125,000 acres of the range in "poor or very poor" condition, but a recently released forest plan nonetheless calls for increased grazing of cattle and sheep on the Targhee where grazing fees for a cow-calf amount to only $2.01 per month, a fraction of what ranchers pay to graze on private land.

Other threats to the Greater Yellowstone Ecosystem are less subtle. Poaching of wildlife is now a serious problem inside and outside Yellowstone Park. Grizzly bears and bighorn sheep bring thousands of dollars per animal on the illegal market, and a rack of elk antlers in velvet can fetch a hundred dollars per pound. Penalties for poaching are still pitifully low and law enforcement is expensive. The U.S. Fish and Wildlife Service has only two enforcement agents to cover an area twice the size of the Greater Yellowstone Ecosystem. And in Cooke City, Montana a restaurant owner has deliberately fed garbage to grizzly bears over an extended period virtually assuring the ultimate demise of the spoiled bears as they come into contact with people on their garbage forays. Severe and widespread damage to many public and private lands in the Greater Yellowstone area also is inflicted each year by careless drivers of off-road vehicles.

Yet another threat to the ecosystem comes from outdoor enthusiasts who are visiting the back country in ever-larger numbers and are simply "loving it to death." In 1982, for example, the back country of the Absaroka-Beartooth Wilderness was subjected to 393,000 visitor days of use, making it the fourth most heavily visited wilderness in America. One portion of the wilderness just north of the Yellowstone Park boundary has an early elk hunt that attracts two dozen outfitters and their clients and more than a thousand other hunters into one small area of the back country.

Upper Gardiner River. (Charles Kay)

Monday, September 19, 1870...We had within a distance of fifty miles seen what we believed to be the greatest wonders on the continent...

NATHANIEL P. LANGFORD

Threatened and Endangered Species: Why Should We Care?

At least 16 species of wildlife are considered to be rare, threatened, or in immediate danger of becoming extinct within the Greater Yellowstone Ecosystem. The area is home to four species of birds and mammals that have been designated as threatened or endangered under the provisions of the Endangered Species Act of 1973. Threatened species are defined as those that are likely to become endangered in the foreseeable future and include the grizzly bear and the bald eagle. Endangered species are those that are threatened with extinction throughout all or a significant portion of their range. In Yellowstone, the wolf and the peregrine falcon are listed as endangered.

With the possible exception of the wolf and the fisher (both of which may be extinct in Greater Yellowstone), these birds and animals still inhabit Yellowstone Park proper. But the fact that they exist doesn't mean that they find prime habitat there. Most of the wildlife species in the Yellowstone area once ranged far beyond, and are now compressed into an area that in terms of their historic range is small and does not provide optimum habitat. For bald and golden eagles, elk, grizzly bear, trumpeter swan, whooping crane, white pelican, bison, cougar and others, Yellowstone Park is too small; even the much larger Greater Yellowstone Ecosystem provides only marginal range. But it is now their only range, and for some of these creatures, the Greater Yellowstone area may be their last chance.

The Greater Yellowstone Ecosystem presents one of the two best chances in the lower 48 states for the survival of the grizzly bear in the wild. (Alan Carey)

Why should we care? Why should we concern ourselves with the needs of a few uncommon birds and animals? What will be lost if they should pass into extinction? The answer to this last question is that we don't know what will be lost. Biologists of the U.S. Fish and Wildlife Service tell us in their publication, Endangered Means There's Still Time, that we are still largely ignorant of the complex ecological relationships that exist among living things in any given ecosystem. What we do know, however, tells us that each species occupies a special niche and fulfills a unique role in its ecosystem, presenting the potential of a chain reaction among all organisms with the loss of just one.

We also know that each species contains a reservoir of unique genetic material that has taken millions of years to evolve. For all of man's genius, he has not yet learned to retrieve or re-create this genetic material, once lost.

Why should we care? We should care because the chemical secrets held in the earth's organisms have benefited man enormously and promise to benefit us even more in the years ahead. If a fungus known as Penicillium notatum had been wiped out, there would be no penicillin and perhaps none of the family of antibiotics that came in its wake. The exciting discovery that snails and mollusks are immune to cancer has triggered biological research in the hope that an understanding of this immunity can be applied to the prevention and cure of cancer in man.

There are other ways in which man will benefit by preserving the earth's life forms. Endangered species are environmental indicators, early (or perhaps late) warning systems that our management of the planet is not working well, that certain life forms simply can't live here any more, and that other species that depend upon the disappearing organisms are also in danger. Man is not exempt from this threat—and neither will he be the last to go.

Then too, there are those who would argue for the protection of living organisms on the grounds that the widest possible range of diversity in plant and animal life simply makes our world a more interesting place.

In the entire 3,000 years before the arrival of the white man in North America, less than a hundred species of birds and mammals (including such creatures as the mastadon and the sabre-tooth cat) became extinct. Yet in the 350 years since we arrived more than 500 species and subspecies of animals and plants have disappeared—an average of more than 140 species per century; and the trend toward extinction has accelerated dramatically in the most recent century.

Should we care? If we do, for whatever reason, we must insist with all the vigor we can collectively command that the area in and around Yellowstone be protected against further encroachments upon the wildlife species that find their homes there.

I have found a pervasive conviction among staff that the most immediate necessity is to return the running of the park service to the professionals.

ROBERT CAHN, AUDUBON SOCIETY

Author's Epilogue: Bad Omens from Washington

With the coming to office of the Reagan administration in 1981, the management of America's public lands has undergone a dramatic change in course. The orientation of the present administration toward resource management has departed so sharply from that of its predecessors, Republican and Democrat alike, that it must be counted as perhaps the greatest threat of all to the wild lands of Greater Yellowstone. The resource management attitude of the administration has been quickly and effectively translated into policies and actions, many of which will last long after the passing of the present administration, and others which are simply irreversible.

Minerva Terrace travertine formation, Mammoth Hot Springs, Yellowstone National Park. (Fred Hirschmann)

Clear-cut logging on the Targhee National Forest along Yellowstone Park's western boundary. (Fred Hirschmann)

This new orientation toward public land management has manifested itself in several ways that are particularly relevant for the Greater Yellowstone Ecosystem. Former Secretary Watt and his associates in the Department of the Interior noted repeatedly that they did not intend to drill, mine, log or otherwise exploit existing national parks. In this, of course, they have no choice, for such activities within the parks are already precluded by federal law. But administration officials have been conspicuously silent about threats to the parks from surrounding lands, and understandably so, for it is here that their closest allies, the corporate energy giants, the powerful timber industry, the stockgrowers associations, the mining industry and other commodity-producing enterprises are so actively at work.

The administration, speaking through the Department of the Interior, which is responsible for America's national parks, has promoted the belief that national parks are islands, that they can stand alone, and that what happens beyond their boundaries is not relevant to the environmental integrity of the parks themselves. The purpose of this strategy is to keep the eyes of the American public inside the parks.

Former Secretary Watt insisted that hotels, restaurants, roads, utilities and other facilities in the national parks were in a "shameful condition." But, while it is true that some facilities in some parks are dilapidated and do need attention, this is an entirely separate concern from preservation of the natural environment of the parks. A case certainly can be made that the facility renovation should go forward, but it should proceed in addition to wild land preservation, not in lieu of it.

The essence of our national parks is wild land, not facilities, and a policy that ignores massive threats to the natural condition of these wild lands while concentrating on facility construction and renovation should be carefully examined. Of what value would Yellowstone National Park be with beautiful, modern hotels and restaurants, high-standard roads, modern administrative offices and remodeled buildings if it lacked free-ranging wildlife populations, naturally functioning biosystems, clean air and water and vast stretches of unmolested wild lands? We may be able to have both, but until the preservation of the wild-land resource itself is assured, we may want to consider making that our first priority. We can fill chuck-holes and remodel hotels any time, but if we lose the grizzly or dry up the geysers, they are gone forever. Once the American public discerns the importance of the ecosystem concept in the Greater Yellowstone area, their concern will begin to extend beyond the park where

they will raise difficult questions about the trade-offs between varying levels of resource consumption and resource conservation.

The same strategy that seeks to keep our eyes fixed inside the parks also is being used by the administration in an attempt to convince Americans that we have enough national parks and public wild lands in our country, that we cannot take care of those we do have and that there should therefore be no more parks and no additions to existing parks.

The Land and Water Conservation Fund was created by Congress in 1965 to utilize government funds, mainly from off-shore oil revenues, for the purposes of park land acquisition. Congress subsequently provided $700 million a year for the fund. Since it was created it has been used to acquire 1.7 million acres of systems. When Secretary Watt took office the fund had more than $1 billion, but he immediately placed a moratorium on further park land acquisition and proposed that Congress return $80 million, which already had been appropriated for purchase of park lands, to the national treasury. He then proposed that the Carter administration's 1982 budget for park land acquisition of $234 million be cut to $29 million. When the Reagan administration assumed office the National Park Service had identified 433,000 acres of private land inside existing national parks to be purchased by the government at a cost of $800 million. Former Secretary Watt blocked those purchases. He also sought legislation that would allow him to divert Land and Water Conservation Fund monies from park land acquisition to his park facility program.

In this and other schemes aimed at preventing the acquisition of new park lands, Congress has partially confounded the administration by appropriating acquisition money, which Secretary Watt refused to spend, and rejecting proposals to release Land and Water Conservation Fund dollars for other than park land acquisition. The former Secretary has in turn foiled congressional intent to acquire new park lands through a series of administrative actions.

In 1982 the House of Representatives showed its dissatisfaction with the administration's attempt to ignore threats to national parks from adjacent lands, when it passed the National Park Protection Act by a margin of 319 to 84. The bill was opposed vigorously by the Reagan administration and by oil and mining industry lobbyists and was killed by the Republican committee leadership when it reached the Senate. An identical bill passed the House in October, 1983 by a vote of 321 to 82, but it again seems assured of poor prospects in the Senate at this writing.

The National Park Protection Act is a response to the State of the Parks Report (discussed at the beginning of this chapter). It provides that federal agencies that are: "...conducting or supporting activities within or adjacent to any unit of the national park system shall, to the extent practicable, undertake to ensure that those activities will not significantly degrade the natural or cultural resources or values for which the unit was established." The bill also would require the National Park Service to submit a State of the Parks report to Congress every two years detailing threats to the parks.

While the National Park Protection Act was passed overwhelmingly by the House of Representatives, it is sobering testimony to the political power of the timber, mining, oil and gas and livestock interests of the west that with one exception, (Representative Pat Williams of Montana) every congressman from Wyoming, Idaho and Montana voted against the bill in the 97th Congress.

The bill also was opposed by Russell Dickenson, director of the National Park Service, who said the bill would reduce the resource manager's flexibility, encourage uncertainty

Gibbon Meadow on an October morning. (Jeff Gnass)

I refuse to believe that the American people enter their parks primarily in search of motel rooms and hamburger stands, souvenir shops and filling stations, snowmobile trails and tennis courts. They come and bring their children with them, to find something much more important: a kinship with the natural world around them, the awe which comes when human beings are in the presence of the majestic beauty created by the forces which shaped this planet.

CECIL ANDRUS, FORMER SECRETARY OF INTERIOR

For the cost of one nuclear aircraft carrier, we could clear up the entire backlog of authorized and uncompleted land acquisitions in the entire national park system.

REP. JOHN SEIBERLING, 1982

Dawn at Eagle Creek Meadows in the Washakie Wilderness. (Ralph Maughan)

and litigation, and perhaps even protect the parks at the expense of all other needs and values. It is at first glance difficult to understand how the director of the agency charged with protection of our national parks would testify against the bill. It is also difficult to understand why the National Park Service has maintained such silence about the 1980 State of the Parks Report and why threats to the park are not openly discussed among park service personnel.

These anomalies are understandable only when it is recognized how highly politicized the Department of the Interior and the National Park Service have become since 1981. Prior to the advent of the current admin-

istration, the deputy director of the National Park Service as well as the associate and assistant directors in the Washington office were typically career park-service professionals. At the time of this writing, only one of those positions is occupied by a career professional (two other positions are held on an acting basis by park-service people). In the spring of 1983 Secretary Watt announced that five of the top-level managers in the park service would be transferred to other agencies. Career professionals are no longer in charge at the National Park Service.

A step above the deputy director of the National Park Service, the Reagan appointee to the office of Assistant Secretary of the Inte-

rior for Fish, Wildlife and Parks, to which the National Park Service answers, is a former oil-company geologist. His special assistant, who exercises broad influence over the National Park Service, is a former employee of the National Inholders Association, an organization of persons who own property inside national parks. Politicizing the upper echelons of the National Park Service has caused regional officials, park superintendents and other park employees to speak cautiously or not at all about threats to the parks.

This long and distressing list of developments, activities and policies that so threaten the Greater Yellowstone Ecosystem tends to overwhelm and discourage those who share concern about the future of the area. This is, however, not the time to give up. Efforts directed at wildland preservation in Greater Yellowstone are more vital today than any time in the recent past. Not only is the magnitude of threats greater, but in many cases they forebode deeper and longer lasting impacts than man's earlier activities in the area. In some cases, the damage they portend is simply irreversible.

This is also not the time to give up because there are some hopeful signs that should give us encouragement and strengthen our resolve to protect what is left of Greater Yellowstone. The first of these is that Congress, for whatever it can do, is not likely to acquiesce to the large-scale degradation of our parks and wildlands. A long history of bipartisan congressional concern for conservation will survive the coming and going of presidents and their cabinets.

The second is that there is in America a strong conservation tradition, a tradition that will not be easily broken. It is ironic that today, at a time when the voices of conservation have so little influence in the Reagan administration, the American public seems more concerned than ever about our diminishing wild lands. This is perhaps partly attributable to a growing awareness in America that as we finish the final quarter of the 20th Century, we indeed are down to the last natural remnants of the earth.

The third hopeful sign is found in a developing awareness among both federal resource managers and the public about the inestimable value of the Greater Yellowstone Ecosystem as a natural area and its fragility and susceptibility to disruption. This awareness is beginning to be translated into action. In 1983 a new organization, The Greater Yellowstone Coalition, was formed to deal specifically with the problems described in this book. The organization is a coalition of groups seeking to

Slough Creek. Yellowstone National Park. (Charles Kay)

promote understanding of the ecosystem concept in the Greater Yellowstone area and encouraging public agencies to make resource management decisions based on ecosystem-wide considerations. At the agency level some small steps have already been taken to do this. Park superintendents and forest supervisors schedule occasional joint meetings, and more formal arrangements such as those relating to grizzly bear and elk management have been agreed upon between agency heads.

Beyond these beginnings much remains to be done. In the end, what is needed is a mechanism for managing the ecosystem as an ecosystem with decisions being based on

sound biological grounds and area-wide considerations. One way of partially accomplishing this might be to consolidate all federal lands in the Greater Yellowstone Ecosystem under one management agency and one management plan. The creation of a National Recreation Area or some other type of congressionally-established, special-management unit may be necessary to accomplish this. That would not come easily. The inertia of old attitudes and special interests is powerful, and the issues are large and complex. It will not come at all unless we as a nation decide what is important to us in this area of the west and unless we commit ourselves to it. The choice is ours.

A high ridge of Mount Washburn points toward Hayden Valley and the Teton Range. (Fred Hirschmann)

Stay on this good fire-mountain and spend the night among the stars. Watch their glorious bloom until the dawn, and get one more baptism of light. Then, with fresh heart, go down to your work, and whatever your fate, under whatever ignorance or knowledge you may afterward chance to suffer, you will remember these fine, wild views, and look back with joy to your wanderings in the blessed old Yellowstone Wonderland.

JOHN MUIR, 1898

NEXT IN THE

MONTANA GEOGRAPHIC SERIES

A Study in Montana

THE ABSAROKA-BEARTOOTH MOUNTAIN RANGES

The breathtaking uplift of mountains along the northern boundary of Yellowstone National Park contains more than 25 peaks over 12,000 feet in elevation. That's just the beginning of the story of "The Beartooths." The geologic story of the Absaroka and Beartooth mountain ranges, which contain some of the oldest exposed rock in the world, helps you understand one aspect of this rugged landscape. There is also a fragile side to this craggy land: the delicate alpine ecosystem where survival is a matter of competition against the elements, not against other organisms. And there is the history of the first explorers and the conquest of Granite Peak, Montana's highest mountain. Learn about wildflowers, mountain goats, grasshoppers frozen in glaciers, pink snow and many other phenomena. You'll enjoy knowing more about 2,500 square miles of Montana that looks essentially the way it did hundreds of years ago. By Robert Anderson.

THE MISSOURI RIVER

In the banks of the Missouri River is embodied much of our history, and understanding the Missouri country reveals a great deal about the character of Montana today. Lewis and Clark pulled against its waters nearly 180 years ago and it has been a kind of backbone of the eastern two-thirds of the state ever since. Dammed and impounded part of the way, yet still wild and remote, stretches of the Missouri have inspired some of the most florid prose ever written about a Montana feature. This book captures the romance of the Missouri, shows its diversity, reveals parts of it most people never see and helps us to understand its people and the economic importance of the country it drains. By Robert C. Gildart, author of Montana Wildlife, Number 3 in the Montana Geographic Series.

OTHER TITLES IN PRODUCTION OR PLANNING

The Yellowstone River—by Bill Schneider
Exploring Montana with Pioneer Naturalists—by Larry Thompson
Montana Indians Yesterday and Today—by Bill Bryan
The Continental Divide in Montana—by Bill Cunningham

MONTANA MAGAZINE
Tells The Whole Montana Story

The history, the wild back country, the people, the wildlife, the towns, the lifestyles, the travel — these things are Montana — unique among the states. Montana Magazine brings you the Montana story six times a year in a beautiful, long-lasting magazine.
Its hallmark is full-page color photography of Montana from the peaks to the prairies.

REGULARLY FEATURED DEPARTMENTS:

WEATHER
GEOLOGY
HUNTING
  AND FISHING
OUTDOOR
  RECREATION
HUMOR
PERSONALITY
GARDENING
DINING OUT

Montana Magazine Because You Are A Montanan

For subscription information write:
MONTANA MAGAZINE
Box 5630
Helena, MT 59604

About Our Back Cover Photo
This photographic mosaic was compiled from Earth Resources Satellite Photo passes made from a height of 570 miles. It was pieced together in black and white and interpreted in color by Big Sky Magic, Larry Dodge, Owner.
Commercial Color Adaptation © 1976 Big Sky Magic.

Front Cover Photos:
A. Great Fountain Geyser—Fred Hirschmann
B. Lower Falls, Grand Canyon of the Missouri—Jeff Gnass
C. Elk in Velvet—Tom Dietrich
D. Overlooking Yellowstone Lake—Mike Francis